## FOREWORD

**Unadorned photography, definite colours, laconic texts set in functional type: these are the formal elements Michael Engelmann uses to produce a sign language that is dense, and yet seems nimble at the same time. In the 1950s he adopted a strictly conceptual working method to drive every trace of unsophisticated adulation out of German advertising, with all the nonchalance of a self-educated artist schooled in American advertising practice. Engelmann made a highly personal contribution at a time when there was a sense of a fresh start and aesthetic reorientation between functionalism and pop. This was to change the direction of German graphic design.**

**One test of his radical approach was the prestigious *Who's Who in Graphic Art* in 1962, in which Walter Amstutz first brought individual accounts of the 413 leading international graphic designers together: Engelmann resisted the idea of having his personal signature printed in the book: he was the only person to have his name set in minimalist sans-serif type, thus symbolically refusing the last refuge of artistic self-assertion. Moving restlessly between the visual cultures of the USA and Europe, he absorbed what was necessary with great intuition, and tried to open up a space for the images and language of advertising in which they could be read as positive symbols of a new world that many people longed for. To do this it was just as necessary to unmask the highly individualistic signature as the last traces of traditional craft – the idea alone was what counted. Thus his work marks, with rare sharpness and consistency, the transition to a new approach that postulated the function of the art director, and really internalised it.**

**Engelmann was a poster designer without reservation: his posters and advertisements bring images and concepts together in a monumental, simple and compelling way to make them into signals with strong associative force. In both small and large formats he involves the viewer's imagination and language, directin[illegible] o the fundamentals of visual communication with poetic cl[illegible] ired conditions for this from a contradiction that w[illegible] l rejection of creative compromise and nagging se[illegible] nds danced on the billboards for Roth-Händle for t[illegible] he outlines of a highly esteemed expressive feat wit[illegible]**

**The desire to shed new light on Engelmann bec[illegible] the Berlin Kunstbibliothek's Sammlung Plakat- und Reklamekuns[illegible] the Museum für Gestaltung Zürich's Poster Collection recently acquired large sections of his work from the estate. This suggested a joint publication in the "Poster Collection" series. Unlike the rest of the series, printed matter other than posters has been included, and a full catalogue of Engelmann's work in the Berlin Kunstbibliothek has been compiled.**



Felix Studinka
Curator of the Poster Collection, Museum für Gestaltung Zürich

Bernd Evers
Director of the Kunstbibliothek, Staatliche Museen zu Berlin

2 **Roth-Händle naturrein**
1963

3 **Roth-Händle naturrein**
1960

4 **Roth-Händle naturrein**
1964

5 **Roth-Händle naturrein**
1965

6 **Roth-Händle naturrein**
1961

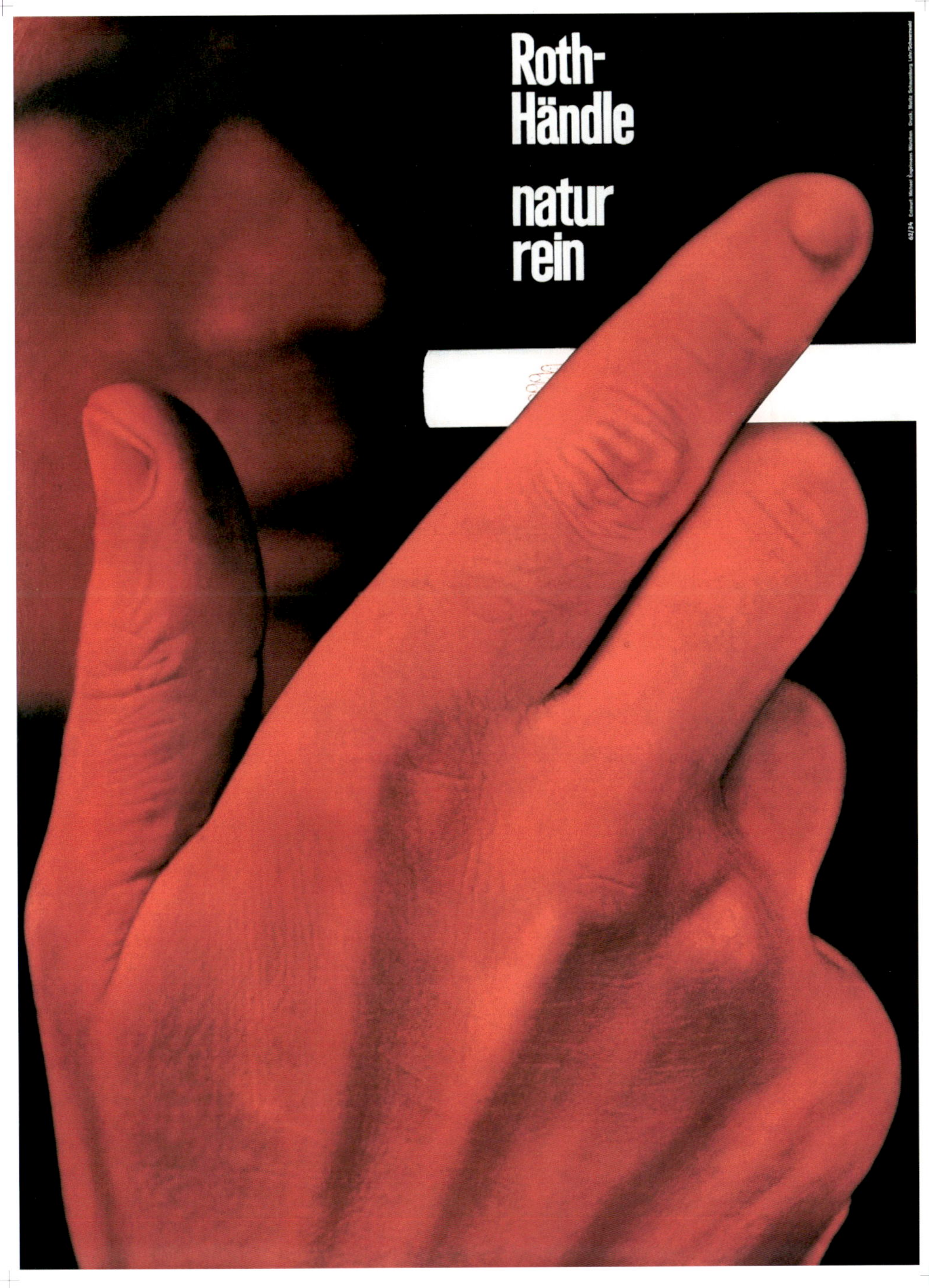


7 **Roth-Händle naturrein**
1962

# REDUKTION ALS PROGRAMM

Anita Kühnel

Engelmann war «besessen von Qualität und Originalität» ein «aussergewöhnlicher Künstler. Engelmann gibt es nur einmal». Mit diesen knappen Worten erinnert sich Pierre Mendell[1] an einen Grafiker, der von vielen seiner Generation und den nächst jüngeren verehrt wurde. Als in Deutschland noch die anekdotische Werbung im illustrierenden Zeichenstil überwog, revolutionierte Michael Engelmann die Inseratseiten der Illustrierten und die Plakatsäulen mit einfachen Bildsignalen und knappen Texten in klarer Typografie. Die mit radikaler Reduktion der bildnerischen Mittel erzielte Direktheit seiner Werbung wirkte ebenso überraschend wie provokant. Jenseits aller auf dem Versprechen eines besseren Lebens basierenden Werbestrategien zielten seine Plakate und Inserate ganz unmittelbar auf das beworbene Produkt selbst. Konsum bedurfte nicht der Rechtfertigung für eine wie auch immer geartete gesellschaftlich determinierte Glückserwartung oder Problemlösung, sondern diente dem individuellen Genuss. Die Klarheit und Selbstverständlichkeit, mit der Engelmann dies vermittelte, war neu. Seine Botschaft traf den Nerv einer Generation, die die Werte der Adenauerzeit infrage stellte und ihre Zukunftserwartung auf einer neuen Lebensbejahung begründete.

Mit dem Erscheinen seines ersten Plakates für Roth-Händle im Jahr 1955 begann Engelmann mit der Popularisierung einer Marke, die bereits damals dank des niedrigen Preises und ihres unbehandelten Tabaks zur Kultzigarette unter den Nonkonformisten avanciert war. Engelmann hat ihr ein Gesicht gegeben, das er über zehn Jahre hinweg mit nie nachlassender künstlerischer Intensität immer wieder neu erfand. Er bediente sich hierfür der Fotografie und wies ihr in der Werbung jenen Platz zu, den die Vorkriegsmoderne bereits für sie zu erobern versucht hatte. In den fünfziger und frühen sechziger Jahren erlangte sie in der wachsenden Medienlandschaft von Print, Film und Fernsehen eine neue öffentliche Präsenz. Sie beeinflusste die Sehgewohnheiten und eröffnete der bildenden Kunst zunehmend neue Experimentierfelder. Engelmann war ein sensibler Beobachter dieser sich verändernden

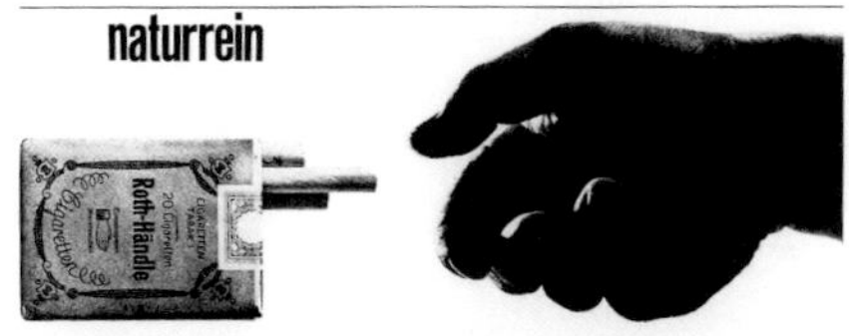


**Die Redaktion raucht Roth-Händle**
Inserat aus:
Die Sonde, Zeitschrift für Kunst und Versuch, Heft 4, 1963

visuellen Kultur. Anstelle der Zeichnung nutzte er früh das bewegte (und angehaltene) wie stehende Lichtbild in oftmals kühnen Anschnitten als Zeichen auf der Fläche. Nicht das objektivierende Ganze, sondern die durch Nahaufnahmen vermittelte Erfahrung ausschnitthaften Sehens wurde formbestimmend für seine Arbeiten. Die darin waltende gestalterische Disziplin und innere Logik setzte neue Massstäbe für die Werbung. Engelmann beherrschte meisterhaft die grossen Formen. Im Kontext intensiver Farb- wie Schwarzweiss-Kontraste sind sie von bestechender emotionaler Wirkung, die bis heute einem positiven Schock gleicht. Diese Werbung ist frei von jedweder Trivialität. «Naturrein» hat geradezu doppelte Bedeutung. Engelmanns Plakate waren in aller Munde und wurden regelmässig in der Presse besprochen und prämiert.

Eine erste Würdigung erfuhr er bereits im Herbst 1950 in der Zeitschrift *Gebrauchsgraphik*. Er war gerade 22 Jahre alt. Wenige Monate zuvor hatte er für die in München gezeigten Ausstellungen *30 Jahre Deutsche Bühnenbilder* und *Amerikanische Architektur im Amerikahaus* Plakate entworfen. Kleinschreibung, Futura bzw. Schablonenschrift, asymmetrische Textanordnung und eine klare Geometrie gezeichneter Flächen verraten den Einfluss des Bauhauses. Es waren die ersten Plakate, die der Grafiker in Deutschland realisierte. Herangewachsen im amerikanischen Exil, war er frühzeitig mit der Ästhetik einer Moderne in Berührung gekommen, die in der westdeutschen Nachkriegsgesellschaft allmählich ihre öffentliche Rehabilitation erfuhr. 1950 zeigte das Münchener Haus der Kunst die Ausstellung *Maler am Bauhaus*, die anschliessend in Düsseldorf und Berlin zu sehen war. Amerikahäuser öffneten den Blick auf internationale Gegenwartskunst und neueste Tendenzen amerikanischer Malerei. Während an verschiedenen Kunstschulen in der Lehre wieder die Anknüpfung an Werkbund- und Bauhausgedanken gesucht wurde, lebte in der Produktwerbung häufig eine in den dreissiger und vierziger Jahren geprägte Alltagsästhetik fort. Hier überwog das Motiv des sympathischen Identität stiftenden Verbrauchers, der eleganten und zugleich modernen Hausfrau, die von Waschmitteln schwärmt und abends Coca Cola trinkt. Fotografie diente vielfach als Vorlage für illusionistische Zeichnungen oder wurde selbst als Trugbild einer idealen Scheinwelt inszeniert.

Es war Engelmanns Glück und Ehrgeiz, Auftraggeber zu finden, die seinen hierzu konträren Intentionen folgten und offen und mutig waren fürs Experiment. 1949 begann er zunächst für die Zeitschrift *international textiles* in Amsterdam zu arbeiten. Es folgten Aufträge für die Kulturbehörden der amerikanischen Besatzungsmacht in München, und kurz darauf fand sich der vierundzwanzigjährige Autodidakt in Mailand, wo er u.a. Plakate für Pirelli realisierte. Ähnlich wie Olivetti bereits vor dem Krieg, begann der Pirelli-Konzern gerade, für einen stilistischen Pluralismus mit hohem Anspruch einzutreten und förderte ein liberales Klima, das viele junge Talente magisch anzog.

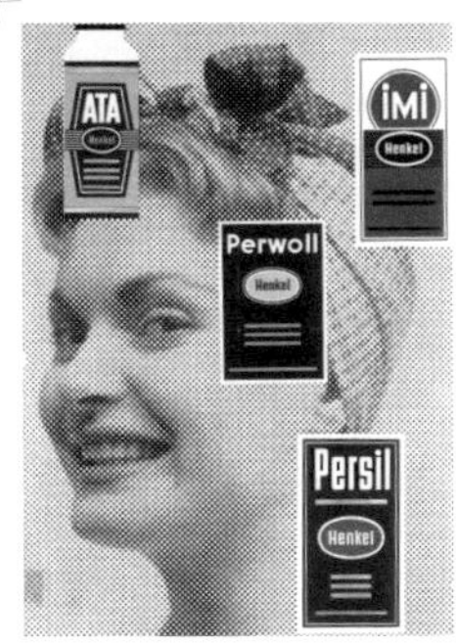


Michael Engelmann
Ata Imi Perwoll Persil
1953/54

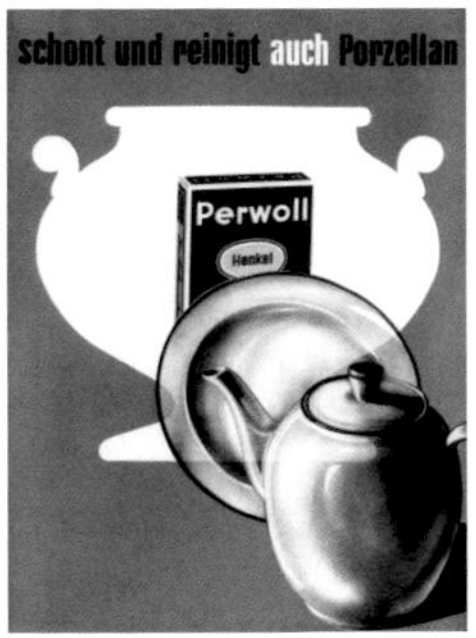


Anton Stankowski
Perwoll schont und reinigt auch Porzellan
1953

Michael Engelmann
Gebrauchte Volkswagen mit Gütesiegel
1953

In Deutschland war zunächst Anton Stankowski ein Vorbild, der Erkenntnisse der konstruktiven Grafik wieder belebte und mit Foto-Text-Montagen komplexe Zusammenhänge sichtbar und begreifbar machte. In der Schweiz erwies sich der Dialog mit Armin Hofmann, Karl Gerstner und Markus Kutter als ausserordentlich beflügelnd. Engelmann bekam Kontakt zu dem Baseler Pharmakonzern Geigy und damit zu einer Kreativität fördernden Werbephilosophie hoher gestalterischer Massstäbe und klarer Botschaften. Er trug sie weiter in die Werbekonzepte für den Parke Davis Konzern, für den er Ende der fünfziger Jahre begann, in München zu arbeiten, zunächst gemeinsam mit Klaus Oberer. Später kam Pierre Mendell hinzu. Beide waren Schüler von Armin Hofmann.

Engelmann verband klare Bildkonstruktion mit Gestaltungsideen, wie er sie in der amerikanischen Werbung verwirklicht fand. Der Pendler zwischen New York und Europa arbeitete 1957/58 im Grafikstudio von *CBS* (Columbia Broadcasting System). Schon im Amerika der vierziger Jahre hatten der freie Umgang mit Fotografie und das Experiment mit Fotografie und Typografie der Werbung ein neues Gesicht gegeben. Abgesehen von ihren wesentlich besseren drucktechnischen Möglichkeiten, die der Fotografie auch den Einzug ins Grossplakat erlaubte, konnten junge amerikanische Grafiker auf einem Fundament agieren, das Bauhausemigranten wie László Moholy-Nagy, Josef Albers, Herbert Bayer oder der Schweizer Herbert Matter begründet hatten. Matter gab mit seinen fotografischen Arbeiten einer neuen Zeitschriftengestaltung wesentliche Impulse. Besonders *Harper's Bazaar*, von 1934 bis 1958 herausgegeben unter der künstlerischen Leitung von Alexey Brodovitch, zeichnete sich durch ein Layout aus, das konsequent die Doppelseite als grafische Einheit betrachtete und Anzeigen wie Zeitschrifteninhalt gleichermassen einbezog. Die unbedruckte Fläche wurde kalkuliertes grafisches Element, das Form bildete und zugleich der Fotografie und dem Text zu höherer Aufmerksamkeit verhalf. In den fünfziger Jahren entwickelten Grafiker wie Louis Danziger oder die für *CBS* arbeitenden Louis Dorfsman und William Golden aus der freien Kombinatorik von Schrift und Fotografie eine neue Zeichensprache aus Text-Bildern und Bild-Texten.

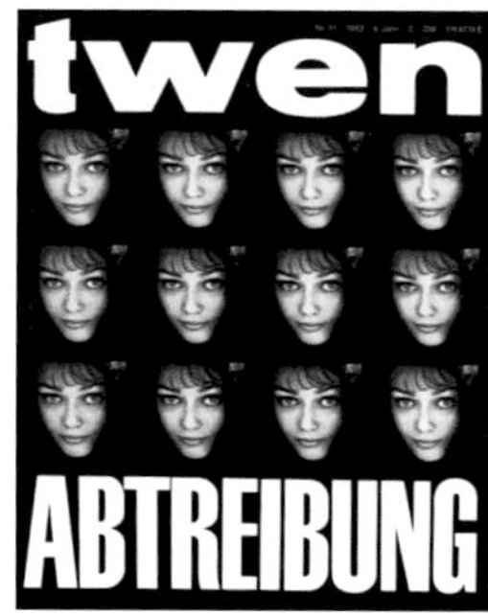


**Michael Engelmann und Pierre Mendell**
**Bols**
Anzeige in Twen, 1961

**Willy Fleckhaus**
**Titelseite Twen**
1962, Heft 11

Nach dem Vorbild dieser amerikanischen Entwicklungen und die neue Schweizer Grafik vor Augen, überwand Willy Fleckhaus in seinem 1959 gegründeten Magazin *Twen* die Grenzen des konventionellen Zeitschriftenlayouts. *Twen* wurde nicht nur Sprachrohr der 20- bis 29jährigen, es widerspiegelte auch die Text-Bild-Ästhetik einer Grafikergeneration, die in Michael Engelmann ihren bedeutendsten Protagonisten sah. Im Spannungsfeld von unbedruckter Fläche, Fotografie und Typografie bilden in *Twen* Text und Abbildung grafische Form. Die Schrift wurde ins Bild gesetzt, Begrifflichkeit im Bild assoziiert. Die Strukturierung von Gross- und Kleinschreibung in serifenloser Schrift und die gezielte Anordnung von Textblöcken im Layout einer Doppelseite ermöglichten eine neue Visualisierung von Inhalten. Fleckhaus holte sich die besten Texter, Illustratoren und Fotografen und profitierte von den daraus erwachsenden Synergieeffekten. Neben Engelmann arbeiteten u.a. die von der Kasseler Schule kommenden Wolfgang Schmidt, Karl Oskar Blase und Hans Hillmann für *Twen*. Zu dieser Zeit hatte Michael Engelmann bereits mit den ersten Plakaten für Roth-Händle Werbeikonen geschaffen, die ihm die uneingeschränkte Bewunderung dieser Generationsgefährten einbrachten.

Schon früh hatte Engelmann auf die Arbeit verschiedener Fotografen zurückgegriffen. Für Libella (1956) 51 und Pirelli (1952) 9, ebenso für eine Volkswagen-Werbekampagne (1953/54), arbeitete er mit Peter Keetman zusammen. Keetman kam von der Bayrischen Staatslehranstalt für Photographie[2] in München und gehörte zu den wichtigsten Exponenten einer Strömung, die der 1951 in Saarbrücken und 1952 in München gezeigten Ausstellung *Subjektive Fotografie* ihren Namen verdankt. Entgegen einem Bemühen um die Wiedergabe sogenannter Objektivität war sie bestrebt, subjektive Wahrnehmungen sichtbar zu machen. Das bedeutete auch Ausschöpfen der Spielräume, die die Einwirkungsmöglichkeiten des Fotografen auf den technischen Prozess der Fotoherstellung eröffneten. Michael Engelmann war von Anbeginn fasziniert von diesen Spielräumen und fand hier schliesslich das Vokabular für seine eigene unverwechselbare Sprache. Früh begann er, sich von einer puristischen Sachlichkeit abzukehren und sachlich im Sinne Tschicholds zu arbeiten, der 1930 schrieb: «Sachlichkeit in der Reklame ist nicht die blosse objektive Wiedergabe des Gegenstandes, sondern der direkte Weg zur Wirkung mit dem Enderfolg des Kaufentschlusses. Auch Überraschungen, sogar Rätsel können daher in der Werbe gerechtfertigt sein, wenn sie die Wirkung durch erhöhte Eindringlichkeit und Einprägsamkeit steigern.»[3]

Engelmann folgte den Grundsätzen seines Vorbildes Cassandre, der im gelungenen Plakat die Lösung des optischen, des grafischen wie des poetischen Problems gleichermassen sah. Mit den Plakaten für *The Philadelphia Inquirer* fand dieses Ideal zu einem ausgereiften Ausdruck. Grossformatige Fotografie hat darin die Zeichnung vollständig ersetzt. Aus einfachen, unspektakulären Bildern wie der Zeitung auf dem Fussabtreter, dem Zeitungspapierhut auf dem Ei oder der Zeitung als Teil des Frühstücksgedecks entstanden klare Botschaften. Ohne Zeitung kann man das Ei nicht essen, den Kaffee nicht trinken und die Fussmatte nicht betreten. Schatten der Gegenstände sind soweit aufgehoben, dass Form zugleich in den Raum und auf die Fläche verweist. Die Anordnung der Dinge folgt im Einklang mit der Schrift einem klaren geometrischen Gerüst. Sie deutet zugleich Szenisches an ohne selbst szenisch zu sein. Darin verbirgt sich eine zeitliche Dimension, die noch stärker in der Folge sichtbar ist.

*Die Neue Zeitung* (1950) 13 ist eines der frühesten Plakate, das konsequent mit Fotografie als Darstellungsmittel arbeitet. Der ausrufende Zeitungsverkäufer ist darin auf seine Hände reduziert. Von einer Hand festgehalten und der anderen anpreisend hochgehalten steht die druckfrische Zeitung im Vordergrund. «Täglich einmal um die Welt», lautet der knappe Kommentar. Schon hier ist szenisches Denken Grundlage der Gestaltung. Engelmann suggeriert darin Dynamik als Ausdruck von Aktualität. Nicht das Produkt, sondern dessen Eigenschaften, Wirkungen und Funktionen werden bildhaft vermittelt.

Das erste Roth-Händle-Plakat 1 zeigt die Fotografie seines eigenen Kopfes. Als weisse Silhouette bildet sie vor den Umrissen des schwarzen Grundes eine dominante Flächenform. Darin sind zeigende Hand und Zigarettenpackung gleichsam Bild gewordener Gedanke. Die Silhouette sollte ein Stilmittel bleiben, dessen Zeichenhaftigkeit einfache grafische Lösungen versprach, von denen so grandiose Plakate wie *Bols* 64, *Libella* 37, 38, *T2* 10 und *Renault* 82 leben. Während die gängige Produktwerbung um die Finessen illusionistischer Bildwelten bemüht war, bediente sich Engelmann einer lakonischen Sprache, die präzise und ganz auf das symbiotische Zusammenspiel von Wort und Bild abgestimmt ist. Gegen die Flut verbaler Versprechen setzte er auf die Unmittelbarkeit des Zeichens. Dieter Fuder sprach in diesem Zusammenhang vom Gestus der Askese: «Nicht benennen, graphisch lösen.»[4] Oft ergänzt Typografie die Darstellung, indem sie die Erfahrungen der visuellen Poesie nutzend, bildhaft wird: als aufsteigender Rauch 79, 80, herunterfallende Asche, als Zigarette 6, 74 oder Rasiercreme 10.

Auf ähnliche Weise wie die Plakate für *The Philadelphia Inquirer* lebt das Bols-Plakat von 1959 von der Balance zwischen reiner Flächenform der Silhouette und ihrem plastischen Heraustreten in den Raum. Der Detailnaturalismus des fotografischen Bildes wird in grafische Struktur aufgelöst, ein Prinzip, das sich Engelmann wiederholt zunutze machte. Weiche Schattierungen differenzieren Nase und Lippen soweit, wie sie als Sinnesorgane Genuss durch Geruch und Geschmack assoziieren. Die Botschaft ist im Unausgesprochenen. Engelmann verfremdet und vermittelt Genuss als intimes Geheimnis. Auch in den Roth-Händle-Serien, wo seit 1959 die fotografierte Hand in unterschiedlichen Anschnitten die Fläche der oft grossformatigen Plakate füllte, wurde das formale Potential der Fotografie kongenial mit den Möglichkeiten der neuen Fotosatz- und Offsettechnologie ausgeschöpft. Fern gegen nah, scharf gegen unscharf wird darin jeweils exzellent ausgespielt. Die Verwendung eines leuchtenden Zinnoberrots, vor schwarzem Grund gegen das Magenta der Zigarettenpackung gestellt, brach mit den Sehgewohnheiten einer um Vielfarbigkeit bemühten Werbung und kam einem Paukenschlag gleich.

Gegen die sich beissenden Rot-Töne setzte Engelmann zugleich die zunächst unspektakuläre Haltung des Privaten: die Hand, die nach der Schachtel greift, zur Zigarette, die sie schliesslich zwischen den Fingern hält. Sie gibt unter dem Blick der Kamera mal mehr, mal weniger Partien in detaillierter Schärfe frei. Engelmann führt uns scheinbar beiläufige Handlungen als monumentale Momentaufnahmen vor und enthebt so intime Gesten des Vorgenusses aus ihrer Alltäglichkeit, um sie als besonderes Ereignis vorzuführen. Er entwickelt hier eine filmische Choreographie, deren Verlauf antizipiert wird, bevor man die gesamte Serie gesehen hat. Zugleich «enttäuscht» er die Erwartungen durch ungewöhnliche und überraschende Bewegungsformen und Farbenwechsel. In dem Moment, wo die Packung aus dem Bild verschwindet, nimmt die Hand deren Farbe an. Schemenhaft tritt aus dem Hintergrund der Kopf des Rauchers hervor.

Auf ähnliche Weise einer strengen Regel folgend, steht in einer anderen Serie die Packung im Mittelpunkt und setzt sich farbig von der schwarzweiss erscheinenden Hand ab. Sie gleicht der Hand eines Magiers, der im harten Bühnenlicht die Packung immer neu hervorzaubert, sie in artistischen Kunststücken in die Luft wirft oder kreisen lässt. Ab 1965 erhält die Hand «natürliche» Hautfarbe. Hyperrealistisch, beinahe surreal tritt sie vor den kaum wahrnehmbaren Kopf des Rauchers aus der Fläche. Hier hat Engelmann ganz auf das Rot verzichtet, das wenig später in der Typografie wiederkehrt.

Engelmanns Roth-Händle-Werbung ist bildliche Übersetzung wörtlich genommener Begriffe. Bis zu seinem frühen Tod im Jahr 1966 erschienen jährlich sechs bis acht Zigaretten-Plakate. Sie lesen sich wie ein gestisches Alphabet der Rauchersprache. Lässt man sie Revue passieren, so erschliesst sich eine Bildgeschichte vom ersten

**Gedanken an den Genuss als Prolog über den aktiven Zugriff zur Zigarette bis zum Genuss selbst. In seinen letzten Plakaten für Roth-Händle kehrte Engelmann das Motiv des ersten um: Die Hand ist nicht mehr im Kopf, die «händelnde» Hand hat den Kopf in der Hand.**

**Engelmanns Arbeiten für Roth-Händle wären nicht denkbar gewesen ohne die unterstützende Haltung des Werbeleiters Cep Portius. Er war es vermutlich auch, der Engelmanns Wunsch durchsetzte, in der Folge Herbert Leupin mit dem Roth-Händle-Auftrag zu betrauen. Mit Leupin begann eine neue, auf anderen Gestaltungsgrundsätzen aufgebaute Erfolgsgeschichte der Marke. Engelmann brachte eine poetische Dimension in die Produktwerbung, wie sie zuvor mit den Mitteln der Fotografie nicht erreicht wurde. Herbert Leupin hatte sie bereits mit der Sprache pointierender Zeichenkunst auf einer künstlerischen Höhe vorgeführt, der Engelmann tiefste Bewunderung entgegen brachte. Beide blieben auf ihre Weise einmalig.**

1 In einem Brief vom 29.8.2003 an die Autorin.

2 Peter Keetman (1916) hatte seine 1935–1937 begonnene Ausbildung an der Münchner Fotoschule in den Jahren 1946/47 fortgesetzt. Die Bayrische Staatslehranstalt für Photographie (1900 als Lehr- und Versuchsanstalt für Fotografie gegründet) hatte ihre Lehre auf eine breite Anwendung der Fotografie ausgerichtet und mit dem 1950/51 eingeführten Fach Gestalterische Fotografie Tendenzen gefördert, die als «Subjektive Fotografie» in die Fotogeschichte eingegangen sind. Als deren Wortschöpfer und Initiator Otto Steinert Anfang 1952 im Münchener Amerika-Haus seine Ausstellung *Subjektive Fotografie* zeigte, betrat er gewissermassen vorbereiteten Boden.
Neben Keetman sind es vor allem die Fotografen Ed Callahan, Klaus Oberer und Wulf Mähl, Roland Reimann und Hans Engelmann (die Namensgleichheit ist Zufall), mit denen Michael Engelmann zeitweilig zusammenarbeitete. Hans Engelmann (1922–1974) studierte ebenfalls an der Bayrischen Staatlehranstalt für Photographie. Von 1961–1974 unterrichtete er hier Mikro-und Makrofotografie, Architektur- und Werbefotografie – Gebiete, deren Anwendung für Michael Engelmann von ausserordentlichem Interesse war. Kontakt zur Münchner Fotoschule unterhielt Engelmann schliesslich auch über Tobias M. Barthel, der ebenfalls hier Lehrer war.

3 Jan Tschichold, Eine Stunde Druckgestaltung, Stuttgart 1930, S. 48.

4 Dieter Fuder, Signale mit Schuss, in: Michal Engelmann, Plakate von 1951 bis 1966, Katalog, Hg. Fachhochschule Düsseldorf 1983, S. 10.

8 **Velocità...sicurezza/pneumatici Pirelli**
**Geschwindigkeit... Sicherheit/Pirelli Reifen**
**Speed and safety/Pirelli tyres**
1952

9 **Pirelli / Il pneumatico che morde la strada**
**Der Reifen mit Bodenhaftung**
**The tyre for roadholding**
1952

10 **Zuerst T2/dann rasieren/viel länger glatt**
**First T2/then shave/smooth for much longer**
1963

11 **Ausstellung amerikanischer Architektur**
1950

12 **Dein Blick in die Welt: Bücher**
**Your view of the world – books**
1954

13 **Die Neue Zeitung/Täglich einmal um die Welt**
**Once round the world daily**
1950/51

14 **Tag des Buches**
1959

15 **Sicherheit? Ja!/Barmenia Versicherungen**
**Security? Yes!**
ca. 1960

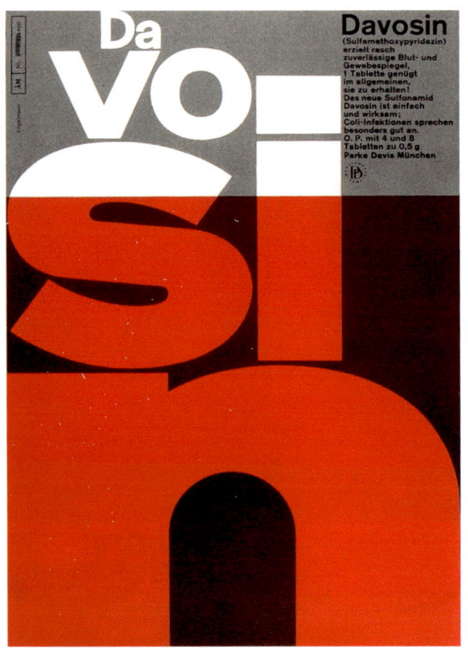

16–19 **Davosin**
**Hepaderichol**
**Benadryl Expectorans**
**Werbedrucksachen für Parke Davis**
1959/60

20 **Chlormycetin Succinat**
**Werbedrucksache für Parke Davis**
1959/60

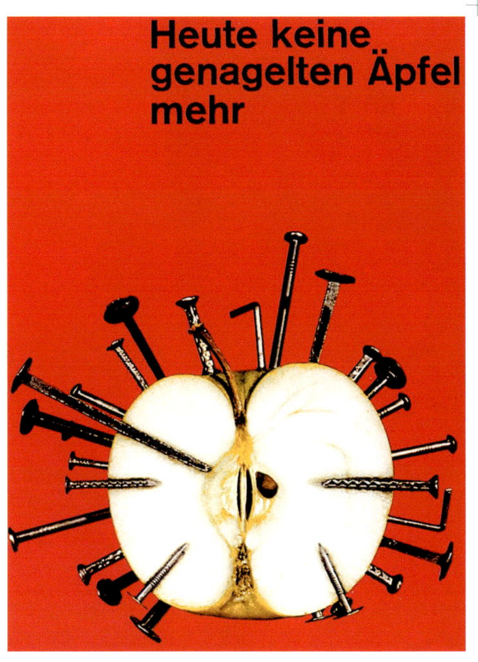


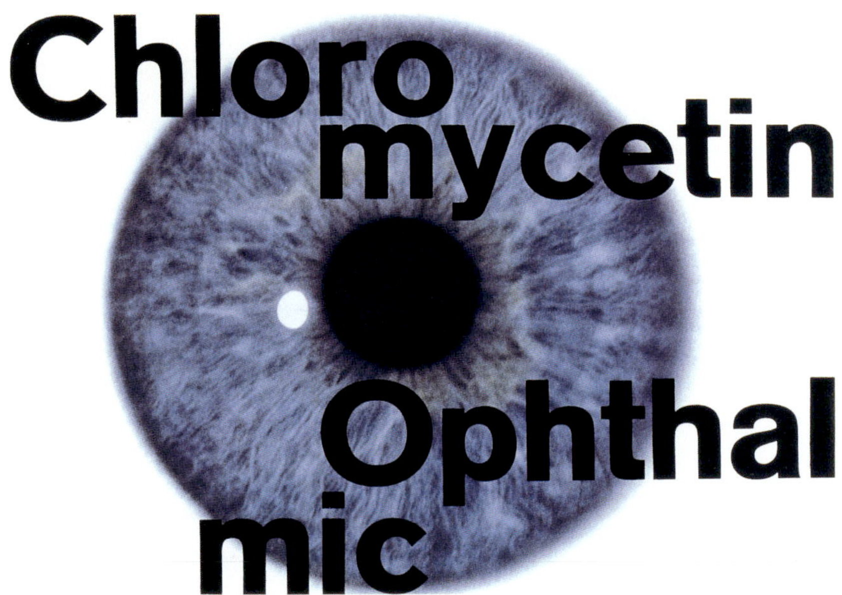


21–23 **Ambodryl**
**Ferrostrène**
**Chloromycetin Ophthalmic**
**Werbekarten für Parke Davis**
1959/60

24 **Kieler Woche**
[Sailing regatta]
1965

25 **Fulda Diadem/Wenn's kritisch wird**
**When things get critical**
Zeitschrifteninserat
1964

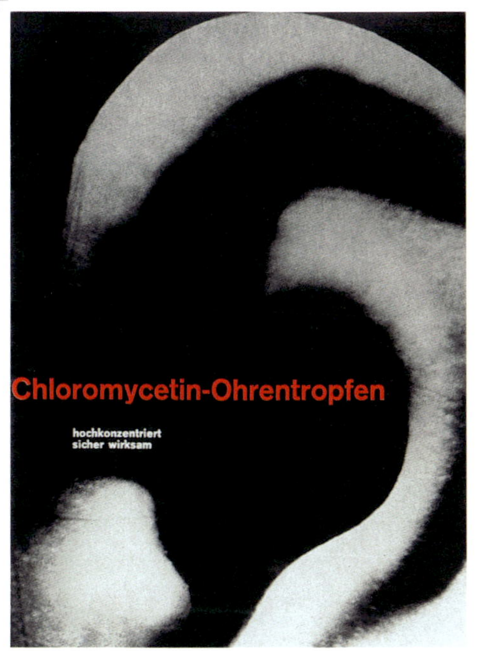

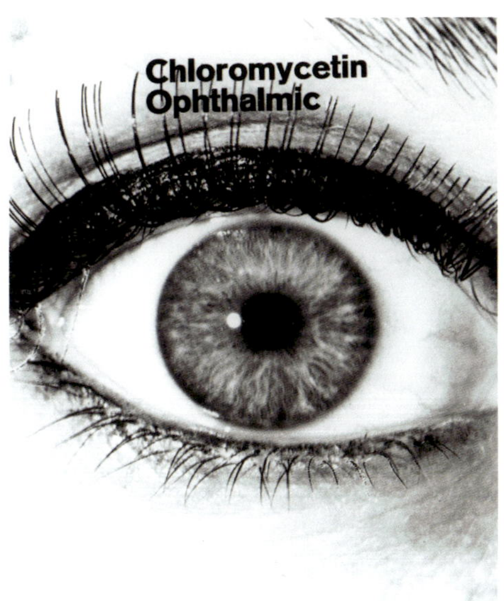

26 **Chloromycetin Ohrentropfen**
**Werbekarte für Parke Davis**
1959/60

27 **Chloromycetin Ophthalmic**
**Inseratentwurf**
1959/60

28 **Pirelli/Il pneumatico per tutti**
**Der Reifen für alle**
**The tyre for all**
1952

29 **Potent Optilets**
1959

30 **Sprich Dü-pi-fiss/trink Dupuis Fils**
**Say Dü-pi-fiss/drink Dupuis Fils**
ca. 1962

31 **Schneller mit Brunsviga**
**Quicker with Brunsviga**
1960

It's for you-
the modern way
of living...
a bedroom phone with
built-in night light

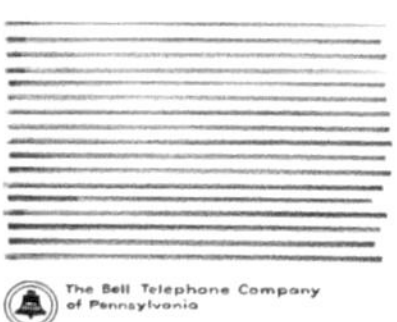

a telephone is
a mighty useful
kitchen tool

your work is
as good as
your bond

Hamilton Bond carries prestige because there is uniform
quality in every sheet. Strong and durable, with a smooth
even surface, Hamilton Bond is genuinely watermarked,
and moisture-proof wrapped for best results in print shop
office and factory. Let your printer show you how
Hamilton Bond can bring out the best in your work!

Hamilton Bond
of course

Hamilton Paper Company, Miquon, Pa. Mills at Miquon
and Plainwell, Mich. Offices in New York, Chicago,

Vice Pr

32–34 **Bell Telephone Company**
Serie von drei Entwürfen, Zwischenaufnahmen
nach Zeichnungen, Silbergelatine
ca. 1958

35 **Hamilton Bond**
Silbergelatine/Collage, schwarze Tusche
ca. 1958

35 **Auch gebrauchte Volkswagen mit Garantie**
**All used Volkswagens with guarantee**
1954/55

Engelmann München

# REDUCTION AS A PROGRAMME

Anita Kühnel

Engelmann was "obsessed with quality and originality", an "extraordinary artist. There is only one Engelmann". In these succinct words, Pierre Mendell[1] is remembering a graphic artist who was venerated by many of his own generation and the next one. When Germany was still dominated by anecdotal advertising in the illustrative drawing style, Michael Engelmann revolutionized magazine advertisement pages and poster columns with simple pictorial signals and succinct texts in clear typography. The directness of his advertising, achieved by radical reduction of his creative resources, was as surprising as it was provocative. His posters and advertisements went beyond all the advertising strategies based on promising a better life and aimed directly at the advertised product itself. Consumption did not need to be justified by anticipated happiness or problem solving, societally determined in some way or other; it was there for individual enjoyment. Engelmann conveyed this with new clarity and naturalness. His message struck a chord with a generation that was questioning the values of the Adenauer era and basing its expectations about the future on a new affirmation of life in this world.

Engelmann produced his first poster for Roth-Händle in 1955, starting to popularize a brand that had even then risen to be a cult cigarette for non-conformists, thanks to its low price and untreated tobacco. Engelmann gave it a look that he constantly reinvented over ten years, with unflagging artistic intensity. He used only photography to do this, thus establishing it in a position within advertising that pre-war Modernism had tried to seize for it. In the fifties and early sixties, photography acquired a new public presence in the growing media landscape of print, film and television. It influenced the way people looked at things and increasingly opened up new experimental fields for fine art. Engelmann was a sensitive observer of this constantly changing visual culture. Instead of drawing, he used the moving (and still) photographic image at an early stage, often boldly cropped, as a sign on the two-dimensional surface. The form of his work was determined by experience of seeing

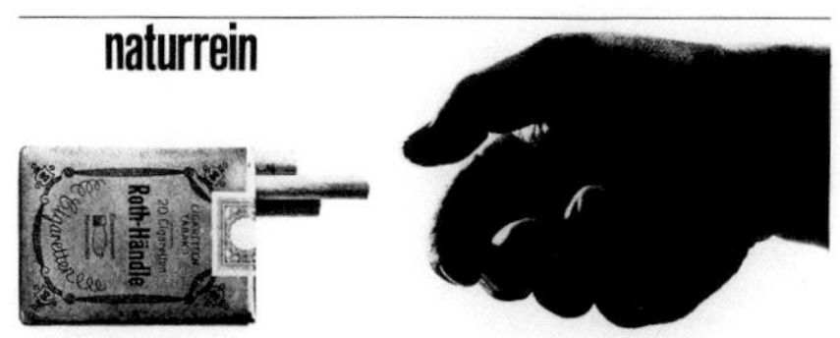


**Die Redaktion raucht Roth-Händle**
**The editorial board smokes Roth-Händle**
Advertisement from:
Die Sonde, Magazine for art and experiment
no. 4, 1963

in detail, conveyed through close-ups, rather than the objectifying whole. The creative discipline and inner logic that prevailed here set new standards for advertising. Engelmann had masterly control of large forms. They make a captivating emotional impact in the context of intensive black-and-white and colour contrasts, and this still comes as something of a positive shock today. This advertising gives not a single hint of triviality. “Naturally pure” almost has a double meaning. Engelmann’s posters were a national talking-point; they were regularly discussed in the press, and won awards.

He was recognised for the first time in autumn 1950, in the magazine Gebrauchsgraphik. He was just 22 years old. A few months before he had designed posters for two exhibitions shown in Munich *30 Jahre Deutsche Bühnenbilder* (30 Years of German Stage Sets) and *Amerikanische Architektur im Amerikahaus* (American Architecture in the Amerikahaus). Lower-case lettering, Futura or a stencil typeface, asymmetrically arranged text and areas drawn with clear geometry show the influence of the Bauhaus. These were the first posters that Engelmann had realised in Germany. He had grown up in exile in America, and had at an early stage come into contact with a Modernism that was gradually undergoing public rehabilitation in post-war West Germany. In 1950 the Munich Haus der Kunst showed the *Maler am Bauhaus* (Painters at the Bauhaus) exhibition, which was shown subsequently in Düsseldorf and Berlin. The Amerika-Haus, which promotes American culture in Germany, was opening people’s eyes to international contemporary art and the most recent tendencies in American painting. Various art schools were trying to link up with Werkbund and Bauhaus ideas again in their training, but product advertising was still dominated by an everyday aesthetic shaped in the thirties and forties. The dominant motif here was that of the consumer who creates a sense of amiable identity, the elegant and yet modern housewife, enthusing about washing powders and drinking Coca Cola in the evening. Photography was often used as a basis for illusionistic drawings or was itself used as an imaginary image of an ideal world of appearance.

It was Engelmann’s good fortune and ambition to find clients who were prepared to go along with his unusual intentions, and were courageous enough to allow the experiment. He started working for the *international textiles* magazine in Amsterdam in 1949. This was followed by commissions for the American occupying powers’ cultural authorities in Munich. Shortly afterwards the twenty-four-year-old, self-educated artist found himself in Milan, where he created posters for clients including Pirelli. Rather like Olivetti before the war, the Pirelli group was just starting to stand up for high-calibre stylistic pluralism, promoting a liberal climate that was almost magically attractive for many young talents.

In Germany, Anton Stankowski was a model at first. He was reviving the insights provided by constructive graphics, using photo-text montages to make complex links

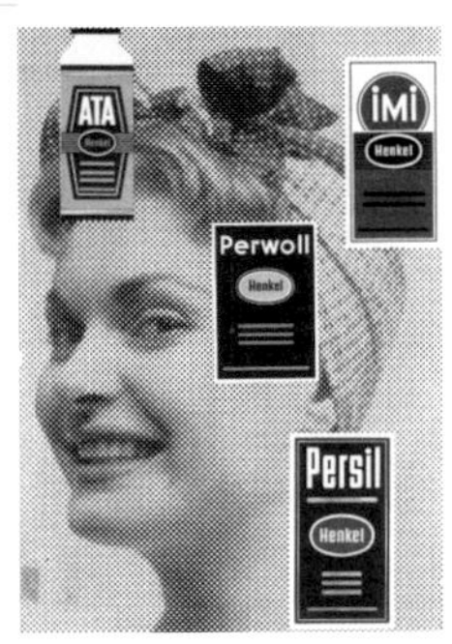


Michael Engelmann
Ata Imi Perwoll Persil
1953/54

Anton Stankowski
Perwoll is kind and also
cleans porcelain
1953

Michael Engelmann
Used Volkswagen with
seal of quality
1953

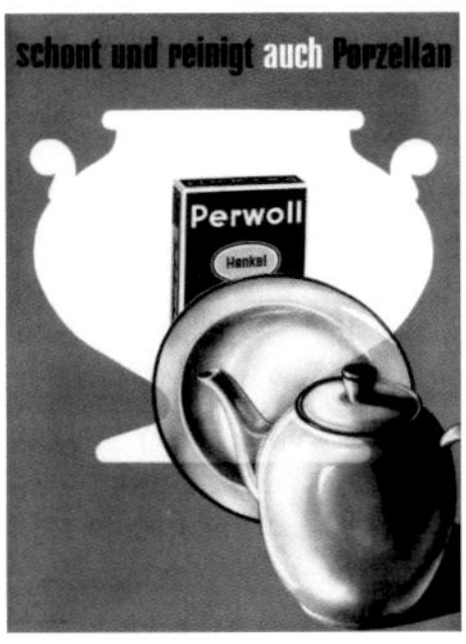

visible and comprehensible. In Switzerland, Engelmann drew extraordinary inspiration from dialogue with Armin Hofmann, Karl Gerstner and Markus Kutter. He was put in touch with the Basel pharmaceutical concern Geigy, and thus with an advertising philosophy that promoted creativity, high design standards and clear messages. He took this further in advertising concepts for the Parke Davis group, for which he started to work in Munich in the late fifties, first with Klaus Oberer. Pierre Mendell joined them later. Both studied under Armin Hofmann.

Engelmann combined clear pictorial construction with design ideas he had seen realized in American advertising. He commuted between New York and Europe, working in the CBS (Columbia Broadcasting System) graphics studio in 1957/58. A free treatment of photography and experiments with photography and typography gave American advertising a new look as early as the forties. Apart from their printing technology, which was significantly better, and meant that photography could be used in large-format poster as well, young American graphic artists could work on a basis established by Bauhaus emigrants like László Moholy-Nagy, Josef Albers, Herbert Bayer or the Swiss Herbert Matter. Matter's photographic works gave considerable impetus to a new kind of magazine design. *Harper's Bazaar* in particular, which was published under the artistic direction of Alexey Brodovitch from 1934 to 1958, distinguished itself with a layout that consistently treated the double page as a graphic unit, including advertisements and magazine content to an equal extent. Unprinted areas were a calculated graphic element that created form and at the same time helped both the photography and the text to be more effective. In the fifties, graphic artists like Louis Danziger or Louis Dorfsman and William Golden, who worked for CBS, developed a new sign language of text-images and image-texts by combining typography and photography freely.

Following the model of these American developments, and with the new Swiss graphics in mind, Willy Fleckhaus overcame the boundaries of conventional magazine layout in his magazine *Twen*, which he launched in 1959. *Twen* was not just a mouthpiece for 20-29-year-olds, it also reflected the text-image aesthetic of a generation

**Michael Engelmann and Pierre Mendell**
**Bols**
Advertisement in Twen, 1961

**Willy Fleckhaus**
**Twen Cover**
1962, no. 11

of graphic designers who saw Michael Engelmann as their most important protagonist. Here text and illustration create graphic form in the field of tension between unprinted surface, photography and typography. Text comes close to pictures, pictures come close to language. Structured upper and lower case in sans-serif type and well-directed arrangement of text blocks in the layout of a double page made it possible to give content a new visual impact. Fleckhaus appointed the best writers, illustrators and photographers and benefited from the resulting synergy effects. As well as Engelmann, Wolfgang Schmidt, Karl Oskar Blase and Hans Hillmann, all from the Kassel school, worked for *Twen* as well. By this time, Michael Engelmann had already created advertising icons with his first posters for Roth-Händle that won him unalloyed admiration from his fellow artists.

Engelmann had used various photographers from an early stage. He worked with Peter Keetman for Libella (1956) 51 and Pirelli (1952) 9, and also for a Volkswagen advertising campaign (1953/54). Keetman was a product of the Bayrische Staatslehranstalt für Photographie[2] in Munich, and was one of the most important exponents of a movement that owes its name to the Subjektive Fotografie exhibition shown in Saarbrücken in 1951 and Munich in 1952. It resisted efforts to reproduce socalled objectivity by trying to make subjective perceptions visible. This also meant exploiting all the scope opened up by the photographer's ability to intervene in photography's technical processes. Michael Engelmann had been fascinated from the outset by these opportunities, and it was here that he finally found the vocabulary for his own unmistakable language. He started to turn away from puristic objectivity at an early stage, and to work objectively in the spirit of Jan Tschichold, who wrote in 1930: "Objectivity in advertising is not just the objective reproduction of the object, but the direct route to an effect with the final success of a decision to purchase. Surprises, even mysteries can thus be justified in advertising as well, if they enhance the effect through increased forcefulness and memorability."[3]

Engelmann followed the precepts of his model Cassandre, who saw a successful poster as solving visual, graphic and poetic problems, to equal extents. This ideal found mature expression in posters for *The Philadelphia Inquirer*. Clear messages emerged from unspectacular images like the newspaper on the shoe scraper, the newspaper hat on the egg or the newspaper as part of the breakfast-table setting. You can't eat an egg, drink your coffee or step on to the doormat without a newspaper. Shadows of the object are reduced to the extent that form seems to point both into the space and on to the two-dimensional surface. The arrangement of the objects harmonises with the lettering to produce a clear geometrical framework. It suggests something scenic without itself being scenic. This conceals a time dimension that is much more clearly visible subsequently.

*Die Neue Zeitung* (1950) 13 is one of the earliest posters to work consistently with photography as a presentational resources. The newspaper vendor shouting to sell is papers is reduced to his hands. The freshly printed newspaper his held in one hand and held up to show it off with the other. "Once round the world daily" is the succinct comment. Here too, scenic thinking forms the basis of the design. Engelmann is suggesting dynamics as an expression of topicality. It is not the product that is being presented pictorially, but its qualities, effects and functions.

The first Roth-Händle poster 1 shows a photograph of his own head. It is a dominant two-dimensional form, a white silhouette against the outlines of the black ground. The silhouette was to remain a stylistic device whose symbolic quality promised simple graphic solutions on which such magnificent posters as *Bols* 64, *Libella* 37, 38, *T2* 10 and *Renault* 82 thrived. Current product advertising was concerned with the finesses of illusionistic pictorial worlds, while Engelmann used a laconic language that is precisely tuned to the symbolic interplay of word and image. He committed himself to the direct message of the sign, against the flood of verbal promises. Dieter Fuder spoke of the gesture of asceticism in this context: "Do not name, solve graphically."[4] Often typography completes the presentation by becoming pictorial, by using the experiences of visual poetry: as rising smoke 79, 80, falling ash, as a cigarette 6, 74 or shaving cream 10.

The 1959 Bols poster, similar to *The Philadelphia Inquirer* posters, thrives on the balance between the pure two-dimensional form of the silhouette and its three-dimensional thrust out into space. The naturalistic detail of the photographic image is dissolved into a graphical structure, a principle that Engelmann repeatedly used. Soft shadows differentiate nose and lips to trigger associations as sense organs suggesting enjoyment through smell and taste. The message is in what is not spoken. Engelmann alienates and conveys enjoyment as an intimate secret – in the Roth-Händle series as well, where from 1959 onwards the photographed hand filled the surface of the posters, which were often very large. The hand was cropped in various ways, the formal potential of photography was brilliantly exploited with the possibilities of the new photo-setting and offset technology. On each occasion distant is excellently played off against near, focused against unfocused. The use of a glowing vermilion red, set against the magenta of the cigarette pack against a black background, broke with the visual habits of advertising that always aimed for multi-coloured effects, and seemed almost like a bombshell.

At the same time, Engelmann set an unspectacular sense of privacy against the clashing shades of red: the hand reaching out for the packet, for the cigarette, which it finally holds between its fingers. Under the eye of the camera, it sometimes reveals more parts, sometimes less, in detailed focus. Engelmann presents us with apparently casual actions as monumental snapshots, thus lifting intimate gestures of anticipated pleasure out of the ordinary, so that they can be presented as special events. He develops a filmic choreography here whose course is anticipated before we have seen the whole series. At the same time he "disappoints" expectations by using unusual and surprising forms of movement and colour changes. At the moment the packet disappears from the picture, the hand takes on its colour. The smoker's head emerges from the background as a shadowy presence.

In another series, similarly following a strict rule, the packet is in the centre, standing out in colour against the hand, which appears in black and white. It is like a magician's hand, constantly conjuring up the packet in the hard stage lighting, throwing it up into the air or letting it circle around with artistic sleight of hand. From 1965 the hand takes on "natural" skin colour. It stands out from the surface against the smoker's barely perceptible head hyper-realistically, almost surrealistically. Here Engelmann has abandoned red altogether; it is to return later, in the typography.

Engelmann's Roth-Händle advertisements are concepts that have been literally translated into images. Six to eight cigarette adverts appeared every year until his early death in 1966. They read like a gestural alphabet of smoker's language. If they are reviewed, a picture story opens up, running from the first thoughts of enjoyment as a prologue, via actively taking the cigarette to actually enjoying it. In his last Roth-Händle posters Engelmann reversed the motif of the first one: the hand is no longer in the head, but the head is in the hand.

Engelmann's work for Roth-Händle would not have been possible without the support of Cep Portius, the advertising manager. Presumably it was also he who granted-Engelmann's wish that Herbert Leupin should subsequently be entrusted with the Roth-Händle account. Leupin triggered a new success story for the brand, built up on other design principles. Engelmann brought a poetic quality into product advertising of a kind that the resources of photography had not previously achieved. Herbert Leupin had already brought it to new artistic heights with the language of emphatic artistic draughtsmanship that Engelmann profoundly admired. Both remained unique in their way.

1 In a letter to the author on 29.8.2003.

2 Peter Keetman (1916) started his training at the Munich photographic school in 1935–1937 then continued in 1946/47. The Bayrische Staatslehranstalt für Photographie (founded in 1900 as a teaching and research institution for photography) aimed its course at a broad range of applications for photography, promoting trends by introducing a subject called "Creative Photography" in 1950/51, which went down in photographic history as "Subjective Photography". When its initiator, and the man who coined the phrase, Otto Steinert, showed his Subjektive Fotografie exhibition in the Munich Amerika-Haus early in 1952 he was walking on prepared ground to a certain extent.

As well as Keetman, the other photographers Michael Engelmann worked with for a time are principally Ed Callahan, Klaus Oberer and Wulf Mähl, Roland Reimann and Hans Engelmann (not related). Hans Engelmann (1922–1974) also studied at the Bayrische Staatslehranstalt für Photographie. From 1961–1974 he taught micro- and macro-photography here, architectural and advertising photography fields whose application was of enormous interest to Michael Engelmann. Engelmann ultimately also kept in touch with the Munich photographic school through Tobias M. Barthel, who taught there.

3 Jan Tschichold, Eine Stunde Druckgestaltung, Stuttgart 1930, p. 48.

4 Dieter Fuder, Signale mit Schuss. In: Michal Engelmann, Plakate von 1951 bis 1966. Catalogue, publ. by Fachhochschule Düsseldorf 1983, p. 10.

37 **Libella mit Schuss**
**Libella Top**
1959

38 **Libella/wirklich erfrischend**
**Really refreshing**
1959

39 **Cinzano**
1964

17 **Grosses Cinzano Preisausschreiben 64 / Machen Sie mit!**
**Competition 64/Just join in!**
1964

41–44 **Jacobi schmeckt mit 18 und mit 80/Jacobi 1880**
**Tastes good at 18 and 80**
Serie. Farbfotografie/Collage
1963

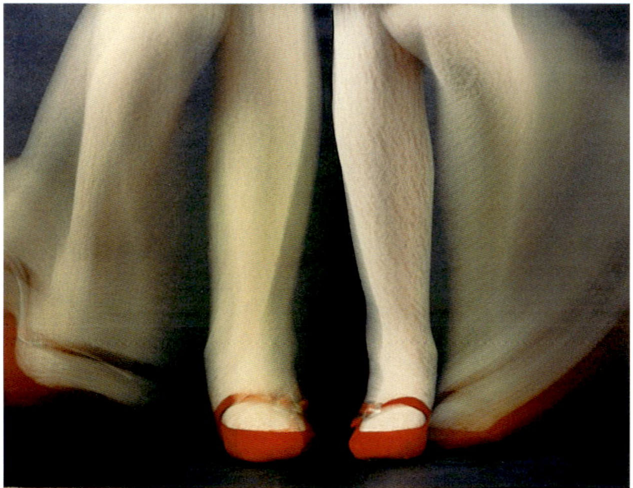

**Danke, o.b.**
**Jetzt fühl' ich mich frei!**

Sie können tanzen, als ob gar nichts wäre. Sie können laufen. Sie können springen.
Durch o.b.Tampons sind die kritischen Tage wie weggestohlen! Das ist gut.
Nur Frauen, die sich frei bewegen können, fühlen sich frei!
Das Jahr hat 365 Tage. Wenn Sie auf 80 Tage verzichten wollen, dann ist es
Ihre Sache. Aber 80 Tage sind fast 12 Wochen. Nehmen Sie nicht doch lieber o.b.?
o.b. nimmt die kritischen Tage fort. Es ist, als ob sie gar nicht mehr da sind.

**Konferenz der Tage-Diebe**

Drei Tage-Diebe. Drei Packungen o.b.
Sie beratschlagen: wie kann man den Frauen
die kritischen Tage stehlen.
Sie einfach wegnehmen, daß sie gar
nicht mehr da sind.

Wer o.b. kennt, findet diese Konferenz ziemlich
überflüssig. Denn schon heute spürt man,
daß man nichts spürt, wenn man o.b. nimmt.
o.b. nimmt die kritischen Tage fort und
schenkt dafür Sicherheit und die freie Bewegung.

45 **Danke, o.b./Jetzt fühl' ich mich frei!**
**Thank you o.b./Now I feel free** [o.b. = tampon]
Farbfotografie (Kodak)/Collage, ca. 1963/64

46 **Konferenz der Tage-Diebe/o.b.**
**The day-thieves' conference/o.b.**
Silbergelatine/Collage, ca. 1963/64

47–50 **Sarotti**
Aus einer Serie von 7 Farbfotografien (Kodak)
ca. 1963/64

51 **Libella**
1956

52 **Good mornings begin with the Inquirer**
1958

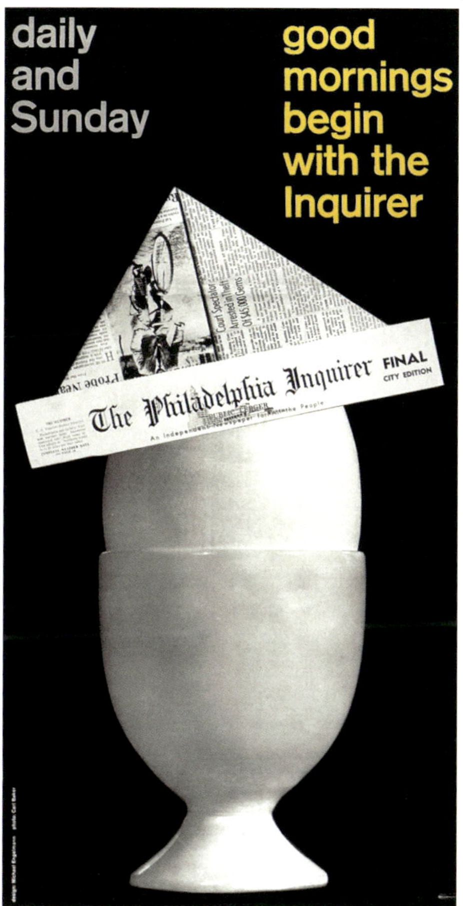


53 **Good mornings begin with the Inquirer/ Welcome**
1958

54 **Good mornings begin with the Inquirer/ daily and Sunday**
1958

55–58 **Im Falle eines Falles klebt Uhu wirklich alles**
**Broken – never rue it / Uhu's sure to glue it**
Serie von Anzeigen
1957

im
Falle
eines
Falles
klebt
UHU
wirklich
alles

im
Falle
eines
Falles
klebt
UHU
wirklich
alles

59 **Das Kinderzimmer**
Illustration zu einer Sience-Fiction Erzählung von Ray Bradbury in *Twen*
Illustration for a science fiction story by Ray Bradbury in *Twen*, 1962

60 **Knud Leif Thomsen: Die Selbstmörderschule**
Filmprogrammheft / Film programme booklet
1965

61 **Das Testament des Dr. Mabuse**
1962

DÄMMER
STUNDE
BOLS
STUNDE

Beginnt der Tag zu dunkeln, sitzen Freunde vereint bei einem Glas **Bols Kirschlikör** oder **Bols Alter Weinbrand.**

Erbitten Sie mit diesem Coupon oder einer Postkarte an Erven Lucas Bols, Neuß/Rhein das Büchlein „Rund um Bols". Es gibt Auskunft über internationale Trinksitten, Cocktails Ihrer Hausbar und geeignete Getränke für jede Bols-Stunde des Tages, alleine oder in Geselligkeit.

62 **Dämmerstunde/Bols Stunde**
**Twilight hour/Bols hour**
Aus einer Anzeigenserie
1959/60

63 **Bols/Gold Top Whisky**
Um 1960
Silbergelatine/Collage

64 **Unverkennbar Bols**
**Unmistakably Bols**
1959

## FREIHEIT DURCH BESCHRÄNKUNG

Auf der plakativen Ebene könnte man Engelmanns Grapheme als Illustrationen von Umberto Ecos semiotischen Abzählreimen für Akademiker betrachten; doch Kunst kennt ein tieferes Gesetz, das Gesetz der kommunizierenden Röhren, das sich jeder rationalen Analyse entzieht. Eine solche Röhre wurde 1947 unter dem Atlantik verlegt: Während Engelmann in New York seine ersten Gehversuche als Grafiker unternahm, würfelte Raymond Queneau *99 Exercises de style* auf die französischen Büchertische. Und wie es der Würfelbecher des Zufalls so will, wird Eco später dieses Buch ins Italienische übersetzen – mit babylonischer Engelszunge. Und diese Zunge würde Engelmanns Kunst OUPLAPO taufen.

Queneaus Buch ist nämlich das Gründungsdokument der ziemlich geheimen Gesellschaft OULIPO: *OUvroir de LIttérature POtentielle*, Werkstätte für POtenzielle LIteratur. Und dank Engelmanns vielhändigen Variationen auch für POtenzielle PLAkate. Im Gegensatz zu den Surrealisten, die sich den automatischen Assoziationen des Unbewussten überliessen, suchten die Oulipoeten die Freiheit im Unfreien, im selbstbestimmten Regelzwang. Nicht die Regeln des Unbewussten sollten die Kreation leiten, sondern mathematische und durchaus auch sprachmagische Kombinatorik. Ein Roman ohne jedes E von Georges Perec oder ein Gedicht von Queneau, dessen einzelne Zeilen man auf 10 hoch 14 Weisen kombinieren kann, denn alles reimt sich am *Tag des Buches* und das Buch sieht aus wie ein Schmetterling, der nach seiner Verpuppung noch zu unzähligen Verwandlungen bereit ist: Zu Hunderttausend Milliarden Gedichten, die gleichsam im Konjunktivus potentialis darauf warten, von einem Leser in den Realis übersetzt zu werden, wobei die Lektüre aller Möglichkeiten, Schaltjahre nicht berücksichtigt, 190 258 751 Jahre dauern würde. So alt wurde Engelmann bekanntlich nicht, doch lieferte er seine Variante vom oulipoetischen Kürzestpoem *T*.

Viele Spielereien der Oulipoeten haben einen Dreissigjahrebart angesetzt, dem auch mit *T2* nicht beizukommen wäre. Doch noch immer verführt uns Queneau mit seinen Spiel- und Stilübungen: Wir steigen mit einem Pariser in den Autobus und stellen plötzlich fest, dass unserer Jacke ein Knopf im Loch fehlt. Und das 99 Mal. Einmal in Form eines Sonnets, einmal als homerisches Epos, wo uns rosenfingrige Strahlen wachküssen; oder der banale Bus bummelt brummelnde Beamte boulevardauf, betonstrassab, jedes Wort mit B beginnend, bevor im scheppernden Blech elende Elemente gen Westen hecheln, entnervt lecke Revers zernestelnd – zuletzt gehen dem Text alle sieben Sinne auf, taktil und gustativ wird die Busfahrt zur Expedition an die Grenzen der Sprache.

Die Beschränkung und Kombinatorik der Elemente auf Hand, Zigarre und Natur-Rein, Rauch-Raus scheint auch Engelmanns Phantasie zu befreien. Das Gesetz, alles beim Wort (*Roth-Händle*), beim Bild (*The Philadelphia Inquirer*), Klangbild (*Dü-pi-fiss*) oder bei der Zahl zu nehmen (*Jacobi 1880*), ja sogar beim bartstoppligen Buchstaben *T2*, die Zweidimensionalität des Plakats als Spielfläche mit immer neuen Arrangements der gleichen Elemente zu füllen, ohne ins Dreidimensionale der normalen Werbe-Suggestion auszubrechen – so sieht Engelmanns OUPLAPO aus.

Massin hat Queneaus 99 Stilübungen einst als Grafiker direkt umgesetzt, Engelmann in Plakate übersetzt. Der Oulipoet weiss, dass jede Ordnung Zufall ist; den unendlichen Möglichkeitsraum verengt er durch selbstbestimmte Regeln. Als Ratte verengt er die Welt zum Labyrinth, aus dem er einen Ausweg sucht und findet – als Literat. Gejagt wird er nun von Engelmanns Plakatze.

Stefan Zweifel

## FREEDOM THROUGH RESTRICTION

At a first glance, Engelmann's graphemes could be seen as illustrations for Umberto Eco's semiotic counting rhymes for academics; but art works with deeper laws, the laws of communicating tubes, and these are not open to any rational analysis. A tube of this kind was laid under the Atlantic in 1947: while Engelmann was taking his first tentative steps as a graphic artist in New York, Raymond Queneau was throwing the dice of his *99 Exercices de style* on to French bookshelves. And as the dice shaker of fate would have it, Eco was later to translate this book into Italian – with the tongue of a Babel angel. And this tongue would call Engelmann's art OUPOPO.

This is because Queneau's book is the founding document of a fairly secret society called OULIPO: *OUvroir de LIttérature POtentielle*, Potential Literature Workshop. And thanks to Engelmann's variations for many hands, also for POtential POsters. Unlike the Surrealists, who gave themselves up to the automatic associations of the subconscious, the Ouli-poets sought freedom not in being free, but in self-defined constraint through rules. It is not the rules of the subconscious that should guide creation, but mathematical and also linguistic combinatorics. A novel without a single E in it by Georges Perec or a poem by Queneau whose individual lines can be combined in 10 to the power of 14 ways, and the book looks like a butterfly that is ready for countless further transformations after pupating: into A Hundred Thousand Billion Poems, effectively in the subjunctivus potentialis, waiting for a reader to translate them into realis, even though reading all the possibilities would take, not allowing for leap-years, 190,258,751 years. As is well known, Engelmann did not live that long, but he did provide his variant on the shortest Ouli-poem *T* by Le Lionnais.

Many of the Ouli-poets' games had a thirty-year growth of beard that not even *T2* could deal with. But Queneau still tempts us with the games and *Exercices de style*: we get on to a bus with a Parisian and suddenly realize that our jacket is missing a button for one of its holes. And that happens 99 times over. Once in the form of a sonnet, once as a Homeric epic, where we are kissed awake by rosy-fingered beams; or the banal bus buzzes burbling bosses boulevard-up, backstreet-down, before the bees are driven out of the words by ees: wretched sheet steel elements eke themselves west, even meeting denested revers etc. – at last all the seven senses open up to the text, and the bus journey becomes a tactile and gustatory expedition to the borders of language.

Engelmann's imagination also seems to be liberated by the restrictions and combinations of the elements in terms of hand, cigar, and naturally pure-in, smoke-out. That is what Engelmann's OUPOPO looks like: obeying the law of taking everything from the word (*Roth-Händle*), from the image (*The Philadelphia Inquirer*), sound pictures (*Dü-pi-fiss*) or from the number (*Jacobi 1880*), indeed even the beard-stubbly letter *T2*, always filling the two-dimensional space of the poster with new arrangements of the same elements, without breaking into the three-dimensional quality of normal advertising suggestions.

Massin is a graphic artist who once implemented Queneau's *99 Exercices de style* directly, Engelmann unwittingly translated them into posters. The Ouli-poet knows that any order is random; he restricts the infinite range of possibilities by imposing his own rules. As a rat, he narrows the world down to a labyrinth, looking for and finding a way out of it – lite-rat-ely. He is now driven out by Engelmann's poster-cats.

Stefan Zweifel


Raymond Queneau, Exercices de style, Gallimard, Paris 1947. Trans. by Umberto Eco, Esercizi di stile, Einaudi, Torino 1983.

Georges Perec, La disparition d'Anton Voyl, Denoël, Paris 1969.

Raymond Queneau, Cent mille millards de poèmes, Gallimard, Paris 1961.

Raymond Queneau, Exercices de style, accompagnés de 45 exercices de style parallèles peints, dessinés ou sculptés par Carelman et de 99 exercices de style typographiques de Massin. Gallimard, Paris 1963.

65 **Roth-Händle naturrein**
1959

66 **Roth-Händle naturrein**
1958

67 **Roth-Händle naturrein**
1957

68 **Roth-Händle naturrein**
1957

69 **Roth-Händle naturrein**
1959

70 **Roth-Händle naturrein**
1960

71 **Roth-Händle naturrein**
1960

72 **Roth-Händle naturrein**
1960

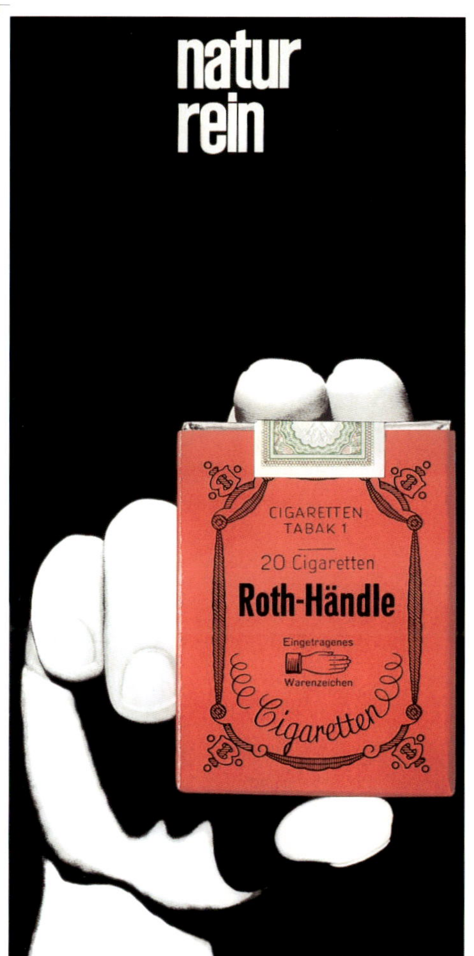

73–74 **Roth-Händle naturrein**
1961

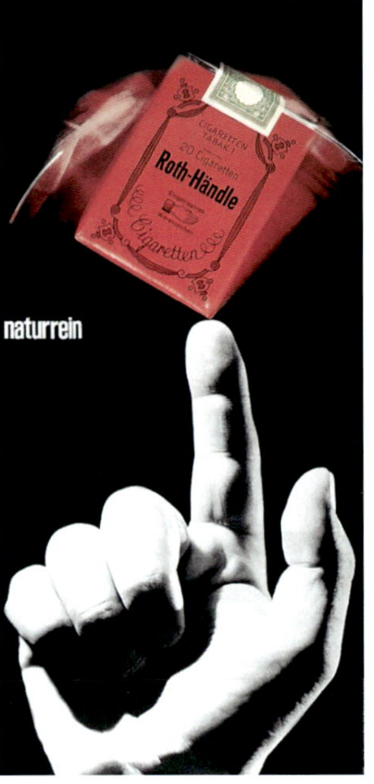


75–77 **Roth-Händle naturrein**
1963

78 **Roth-Händle naturrein**
1963

79 **Roth-Händle naturrein**
1962

80 **Roth-Händle naturrein**
1962

## WERBUNG MIT HAND UND FUSS

Engelmann hat den Antrieb zu seiner Arbeit einmal so beschrieben, dass eine dem Kunden vertraute Sprache gefunden werden müsse, denn nur diese Vertrautheit berühre spontan. Angesichts dieser Verpflichtung stellt sich die Frage, warum in seinen Arbeiten erstaunlich oft der eigene Kopf, die eigene Hand und im Falle des Plakats für Renault R8 82 auch der eigene Fuss erscheint, bleiben sie doch für die vordergründige Werbebotschaft ohne Folge. Doch gerade darum scheint Engelmanns Selbstbezüglichkeit ein Bekenntnis zu jener «vertrauten Sprache» zu erkennen zu geben, nach der er suchte. Gewiss, durch die grossräumige Verbreitung der mit der eigenen Hand «signierten» Roth-Händle-Werbung wurde sie zum persönlichen Markenzeichen voller Anspruch auf Beachtung. Eine für Roth-Händle vorgesehene Serie von Fotomontagen verdeutlicht jedoch, dass er damit nicht Zeugnis seiner Person, sondern seiner Sprache ablegen wollte: Für die Serie wurden die Gesichter rauchender Personen in Engelmanns Handteller montiert, mitunter auch sein eigenes 110. Das Ergebnis lässt an das Selbstbildnis eines Pioniers der Foto-Grafik denken, El Lissitzkys «Konstrukteur» aus dem Jahr 1924. In beiden Fällen lädt die fotografische Überlagerung von Kopf und Hand dazu ein, über das Biografische hinaus eine metaphorische Sinnebene zu lesen. Bei Engelmann aber scheint die Mehrdeutigkeit der Montage als parodistisches Vexierspiel ausgekostet zu werden: Seiner Miene liesse sich leicht ein schalkhaftes Vergnügen über den Husarenstreich unterstellen, zugleich den Sender (durch die eigene Hand), das Medium (als Autor) und den Adressaten (als Roth-Händle-Raucher) mit seiner Person verknüpft zu haben. Dies allerdings mit der Einschränkung, dass die Semiotik, die in diesen Jahren die Werbung zu entdecken begann, für Engelmann ebenso papieren war wie der ferne Pionier Lissitzky. Wenn der unbefangene Einsatz des eigenen Körpers etwas zu erkennen gibt, so ist es das Heureka eines Grafikers, der sich nicht nur an der suggestiven Wucht begeistert, die die Montagetechnik freisetzt, sondern diese auch zielgenau zu lenken versteht. Unter diesem Vorzeichen ist die Renault-Kampagne zu lesen. Nicht die polierten Karosserieteile des Autos, sondern seine Eigenschaften sollten hervorgehoben werden. Folgerichtig ist der Renault zu einem Signet geschrumpft, während die Vorzüge des Automatikgetriebes durch den knappen Text und zwei riesenhafte Schattenrisse evoziert werden und zur Bewertung eines Produkts «mit Hand und Fuss» zwingen. Drei Verkehrsformen der Kommunikation kreuzen sich hier: die Gestik, das grafische Zeichen und die Umgangssprache. Die zweidimensionale Montage wird dabei als Gestaltungsmittel offen gelegt und fordert dazu auf, diese im spielerischen Umgang mit der eigenen, «vertrauten Sprache» zusammenzufügen. Nicht nur in der Aussage, auch im Ausdruck triumphiert die Konstruktion über die Fassade. Engelmann stellt sich so in die Reihe jener «Konstrukteure», die die Rolle des Künstlers für das Werk relativierten. Nicht die Signatur des Künstlers, sondern die Schlüssigkeit seiner Gebilde will hier bewertet werden. Dafür hat er, der ursprünglich Schauspieler werden wollte, das naheliegendste Kommunikationsmittel eingesetzt: den eigenen Körper.

Felix Studinka

## ADVERTISING THAT MAKES SENSE – WITH HAND AND FOOT

Engelmann once described the source of the driving force behind his work like this: a language that is familiar to the client has to be found, as only such familiarity can touch people spontaneously. Given this commitment, we are compelled to wonder why his own head, his own hand and, in the case of the Renault R8 82 poster his own foot appear in his work with such astonishing frequency, even though they are irrelevant to the surface message conveyed by the advertisement. But it is precisely for this reason that Engelmann's self-referentiality seems to suggest faith in the "familiar language" he was looking for. Of course the enormous area covered by the Roth-Händle campaign, which was "signed" with his own hand, made it into a personal trademark with a considerable claim to attention. But a series of photo-montages planned for Roth-Händle makes it clear that it was intended to stand for his language, not for his person: for this series, faces of individuals smoking were mounted on the palm of Engelmann's hand, with his own face featured once 110. The result is reminiscent of a self-portrait by a pioneer of photo-graphics, El Lissitzky's "The Constructor", dating from 1924. In both cases the photographic superimposition of head and hand demands a reading that goes beyond biography to a metaphorical plane of meaning. But in Engelmann's case the ambiguity of the montage seems to be enjoyed as a parodistic puzzle picture: his expression could certainly be said to be taking a mischievous pleasure in the daring coup of having linked the signifier (through his own hand), the medium (as author) and the addressee (as a Roth-Händle smoker) with his own person. Though the reservation has to be made that semiotics, which started to discover advertising in those years, was just as wooden for Engelmann as the distant pioneer El Lissitzky. If uninhibited use of his own body suggests anything it is the Eureka of a graphic artist who is not just enthusiastic about the suggestive power unleashed by the montage technique, but also knows how to control that energy very precisely. This is how the Renault campaign should be read. It is not the polished bodywork of the car that is to be emphasised, but its qualities. Consequently the Renault has shrunk to a logo, while the advantages of the automatic gearbox are evoked by the succinct text and two gigantic silhouettes, compelling the viewer to assess a product "with hand and foot" – "mit Hand und Fuss", in a way that makes sense. Three forms of communication overlap here: gesture, the graphic sign and colloquial language. Here the two-dimensional montage is laid open as a creative resource and challenges us to fit this together in the playful handling of our own "familiar language". Construction triumphs over façade, not just in the message, but also in terms of expression. In this way, Engelmann joins those "constructors" who relativize the role of the artist for the work. It is not the artist's signature, but the conclusiveness of his structures that is to be assessed here. And so Engelmann, who originally wanted to be an actor, has used the means of communication that most readily suggests itself: his own body.

Felix Studinka

81 **Renault R4L / jetzt DM 4.200**
**Now DM 4,200**
1963

82 **Renault R8 / Hand und Fuss sind frei**
**Hand and foot are free**
1963

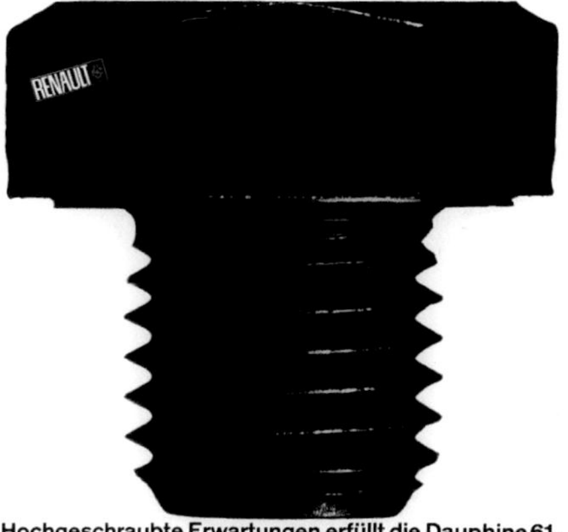

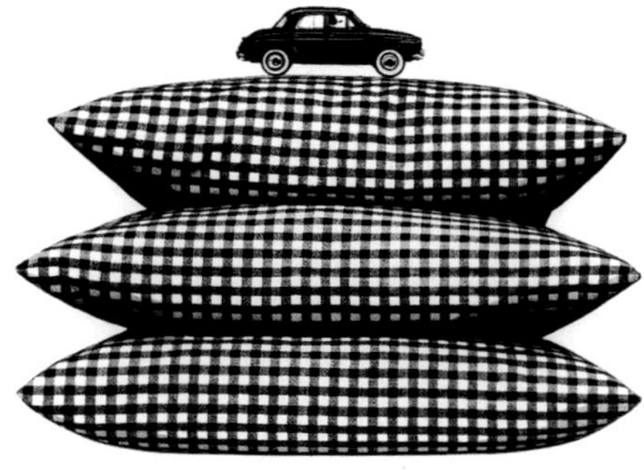

83–87 **Renault-Serie**
Inseratandrucke
1961–63

**1898**

**1932**

**1963**

Drei Generationen bei Renault. Väter, Söhne und Enkel – beschäftigt bei Renault. Keine Seltenheit. Denn schon 1898 wurde das Werk gegründet – an der Schwelle der Technisierung unserer Zeit. Viel hat Renault dazu beigetragen. Als Pionier im Automobilbau. Als Förderer der Groß-Serien-Produktion. Als Schrittmacher der Automatisierung. All diese Entwicklungen ruhen dabei fest auf dem sicheren Fundament der Tradition. Deshalb steht es gut um ein Werk, in dem sich Erfahrung und Fortschritt so ideal verbinden.

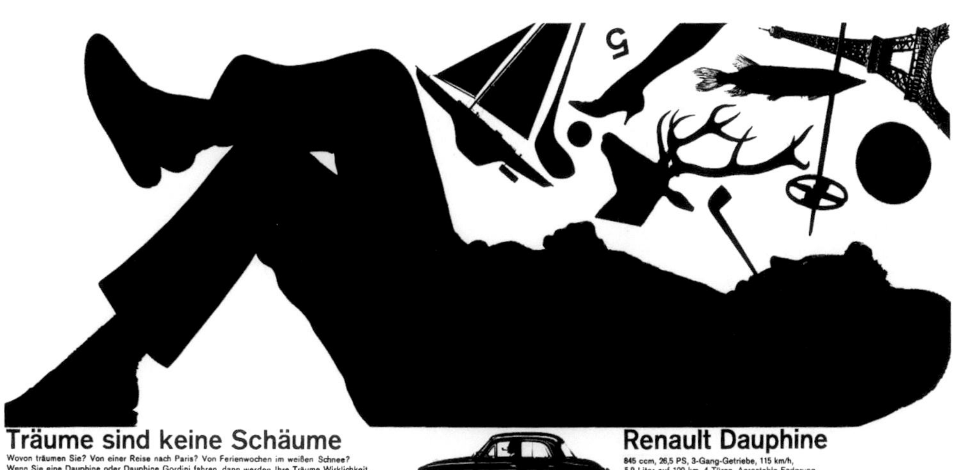


## Träume sind keine Schäume

Wovon träumen Sie? Von einer Reise nach Paris? Von Ferienwochen im weißen Schnee?
Wenn Sie eine Dauphine oder Dauphine Gordini fahren, dann werden Ihre Träume Wirklichkeit.
Denn sparsam sind diese Wagen. Sie nippen Benzin aus dem Fingerhut.
Da können Sie noch manche Mark auf die hohe Kante legen!

## Renault Dauphine

845 ccm, 26,5 PS, 3-Gang-Getriebe, 115 km/h,
5,9 Liter auf 100 km, 4 Türen, Aerostable-Federung,
DM 4798.– ab Köln. Mit 4-Gang-Getriebe
DM 95.– mehr.
Dauphine Gordini: 36 PS, 4-Gang-Getriebe,
126 km/h, 6,4 Liter auf 100 km, DM 5555.–

RENAULT

## 48 Eiffeltürme

Renault ist groß. Aus dem in einem Jahr von Renault verarbeiteten Stahl könnte man 48 Eiffeltürme bauen – fast jede Woche einen. Die Gesamtfläche aller Renault-Werke zusammengenommen ist so groß wie zwei Drittel der Grundfläche von Paris! 70000 Mitarbeiter, mehrere 100000 Beschäftigte in der weltweiten Renault-Organisation. Aus dem Glas der Fensterscheiben der Büros und Werke könnte man eine Flasche formen, in die ganz Paris hineinginge – inklusive Eiffelturm. Paris ist eine große Stadt, und groß ist auch Renault.

## Der schöpferische Geist von Renault

Tausende Wissenschaftler und Techniker im Forschungszentrum von Renault. Millionen Gedanken gehen täglich durch ihre Köpfe. Und das Ergebnis? Ungezählte Patente garantieren die Zukunft. Und – ständig greifbar – technische Lösungen, die richtungsweisend sind. Für den schöpferischen Geist von Renault gibt es viele Beispiele: die vollautomatischen Transferstraßen, höchste Vervollkommnung der Rationalisierung und Serienproduktion. Revolutionäre Neuerungen im Automobilbau – wie jetzt wieder der Renault R4 und der Renault R8. Renault denkt an morgen und bahnt der Zukunft ihren Weg!

RENAULT

88–89 **Renault-Serie**
Inseratandrucke
1961–63

## Ihre Frau muß nicht jeden Pfennig umdrehen

Wenn es jeden Abend Quark mit Pellkartoffeln gäbe und nur sonntags einen Hering, dann würde einem die Freude am eigenen Auto schon bald vergehen. Und eine Frau, die beim Einkaufen Angst vor der Registrierkasse haben muß, ist auch nicht gerade die ideale Beifahrerin. Autofahren – und doch gut leben – das ist das gute Rezept der klugen Leute, die sich für eine Dauphine oder Dauphine Gordini entscheiden! Beides sehr elegante, geräumige Wagen – wobei die sportliche Dauphine Gordini schon fast an der Grenze zum Luxuswagen rangiert. Beide aber von sprichwörtlicher Bescheidenheit im Verbrauch! Nichts, aber auch gar nichts hätten Sie davon, wenn Ihr Wagen bei gleicher Leistung 10 Liter Benzin verbrauchen würde statt 5,9 Liter. Nur ein Loch im Portemonnaie – und eventuell Diskussionen mit der Ehefrau, die es nicht einsieht, warum ausgerechnet sie mit dem Pfennig geizen muß. Wirklich, das braucht nicht zu sein. Gönnen Sie sich und Ihrer Familie das volle Einkaufsnetz – dann ist Ihre Freude doppelt groß, wenn Sie mit elegantem Schwung vor dem Feinkostgeschäft vorfahren, um Ihre Frau vom Einkaufen abzuholen! Für kluge Leute ist nur dieser Weg gangbar. Nur so wird der Autokauf zu einem sinnvollen Unternehmen. Also: gleich mal mit dem Renault-Händler sprechen. Er rechnet Ihnen in DM und Pfennig vor, was man mit Dauphine und auch Dauphine Gordini monatlich sparen kann. Nach diesem Gespräch rückt Ihr eigener Wagen in greifbare Nähe!

Renault Dauphine: Viertakt-Motor, 845 ccm, 26,5 PS, 3-Gang-Getriebe, 115 km/h, 5,9 Liter auf 100 km, 4 Türen, Aerostable-Federung, DM 4790.– ab Köln. Mit 4-Gang-Getriebe DM 95.– mehr.

Dauphine Gordini: Gordini-Spezial-Viertakt-Motor, 845 ccm, 36 PS, 4-Gang-Getriebe, 126 km/h, 6,4 Liter auf 100 km, 4 Türen, Aerostable-Federung, DM 5555.– ab Köln.

**Renault Dauphine**

90 **Renault-Serie**
Inseratandruck
1961–63

91 **Roth-Händle naturrein**
1964

92 **Roth-Händle naturrein**
1964

93 **Roth-Händle naturrein**
1965

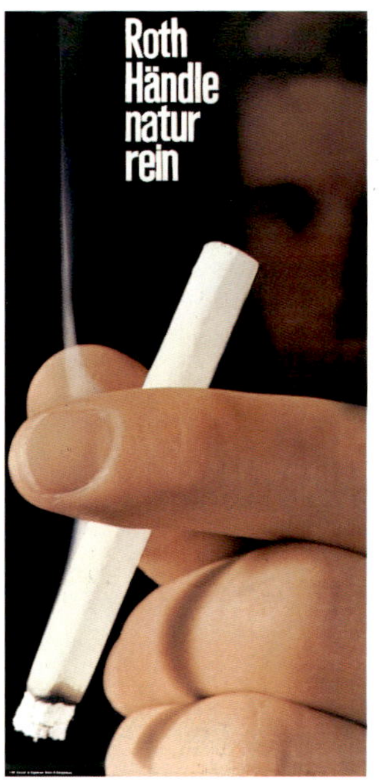

94–97 **Roth-Händle naturrein**
1965

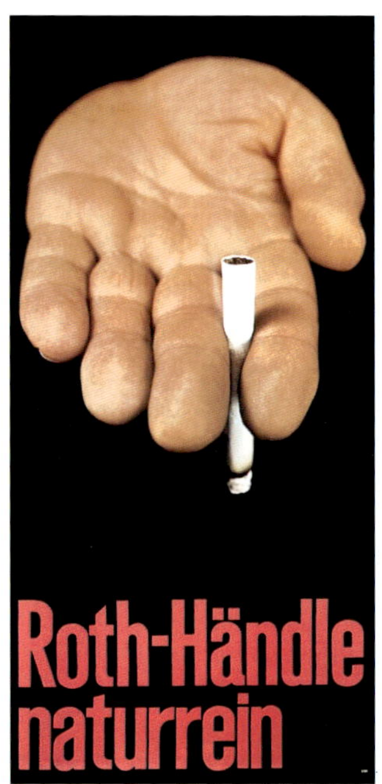

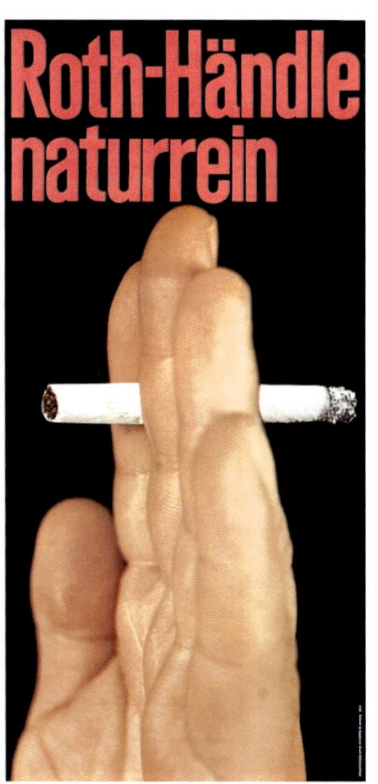


98–101 **Roth-Händle naturrein**
1966

102 **Roth-Händle naturrein**
1966

103–108 **Studien zu Roth-Händle**
Aus einer Serie von 7 Fotografien
Silbergelatine
Um 1963

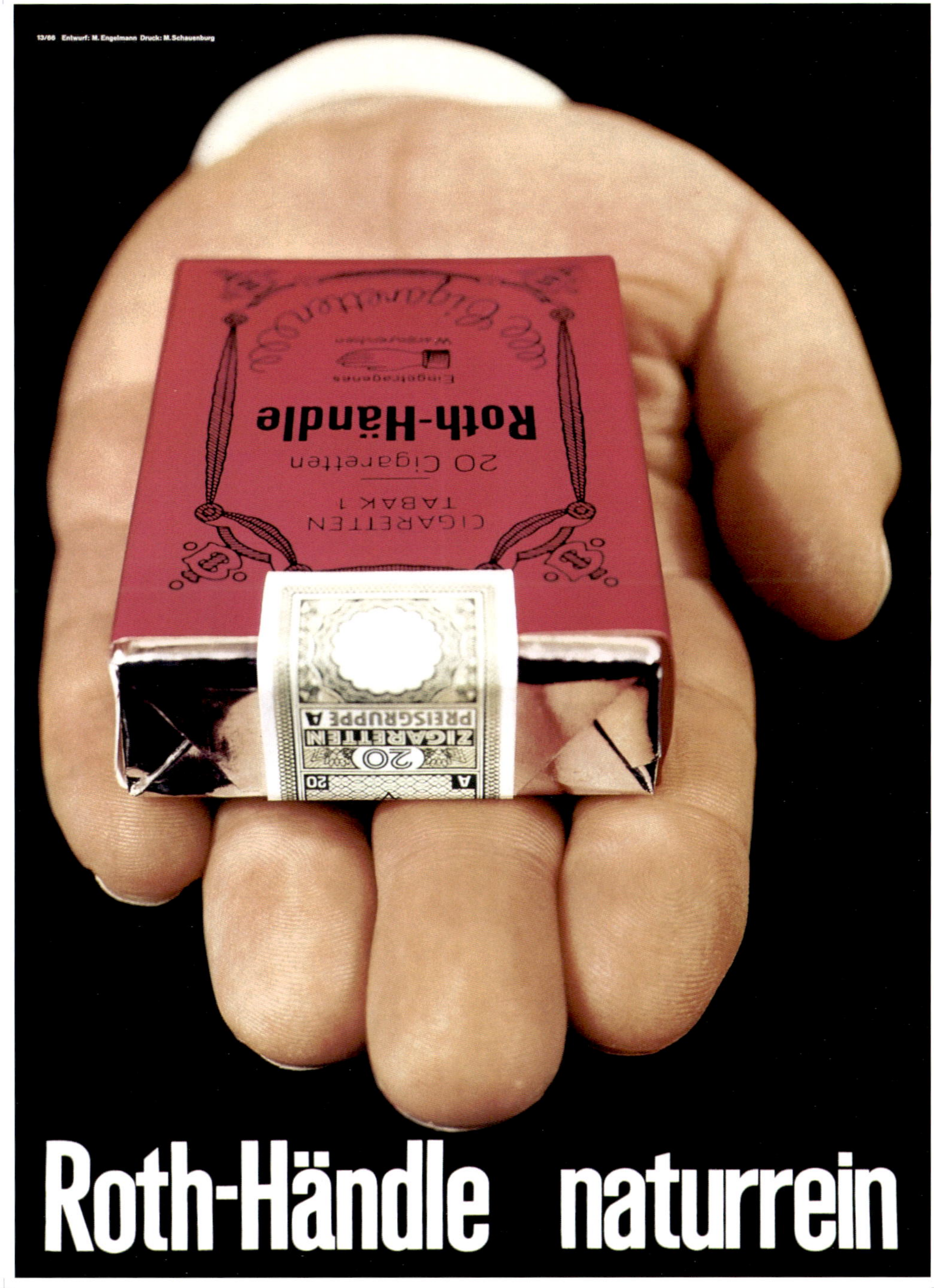


109 **Roth-Händle naturrein**
1966

**Katalog**
Die abgebildeten Plakate, Drucksachen und Entwürfe stammen aus der Sammlung Plakat- und Reklamekunst der Kunstbibliothek, Staatliche Museen zu Berlin und aus der Plakatsammlung des Museums für Gestaltung Zürich. Für die Besitzangabe stehen jeweils die Buchstaben B für Berlin Z für Zürich.

Wenn nicht anders vermerkt, handelt es sich um Plakate.

Bei den Plakaten folgen die Daten des Katalogs den Rubriken Plakattext, Fotografie, soweit bekannt, Erscheinungsjahr, Erscheinungsland, Drucktechnik, Format, Besitzangabe. Dabei gelten folgende Regelungen:

Plakattext: Die beste Textwiedergabe bildet die Abbildung des Plakats selbst. Darum wird hier eine vereinfachte Form wiedergegeben, welche nur die aussagekräftigsten Textbestandteile berücksichtigt. Allfällige Umstellungen dienen der Verständlichkeit. Das Zeichen / trennt inhaltliche Texteinheiten.

Fotografie: Die wenigsten Arbeiten geben Auskunft über den Fotografen. Michael Engelmann hat teilweise selbst die fotografischen Vorlagen realisiert, häufig jedoch mit folgenden Fotografen zusammengearbeitet: Ed Callahan, Hans Engelmann, Peter Keetman, Wulf Mähl, Klaus Oberer, Roland Reimann.

Soweit nicht anders vermerkt, wurden alle Plakate und Drucksachen in Deutschland gedruckt.

Format: Die Angaben werden in der Abfolge Höhe × Breite und in cm gemacht.

Die Plakatgeschichte ist ein junges Forschungsgebiet – verlässliche Informationen sind rar. Jeder Hinweis und jede Ergänzung sind willkommen:
plakat.sammlung@museum-gestaltung.ch und
kb@smb.spk-berlin.de

**Anzeigen und Illustrationen von Michael Engelmann erschienen u. a. in folgenden Zeitschriften:**

Deutsche Medizinische Wochenschrift (1960)
Gebrauchsgraphik (1950, 1957)
Neue Illustrierte (1965)
Quick (1964)
Spiegel (1964)
Stern (1959, 1960, 1964)
Twen (1960 – 1963)

**Catalogue**
The posters, printed matter and drafts illustrated here are from the Sammlung Plakat- und Reklamekunst at the Kunstbibliothek Berlin and the Poster Collection at the Museum für Gestaltung Zürich. The letters B for Berlin and Z for Zurich indicate which organization owns the item.

The items are posters unless identified otherwise.

For the posters, the information in the catalogue follows this order: poster text, photographer, year of appearance, country of appearance, printing technique, format, ownership. The following rules are followed:

Poster text: the illustration of the poster itself provides the best version of the text. Hence a simplified form is given here, featuring only key sections of the text. Any rearrangement is to facilitate understanding. The sign / separates text units in terms of content.

Photography: only a very few of the works provide information about the photographer. Michael Engelmann took some of the photographs he used himself, but frequently worked with the following photographers: Ed Callahan, Hans Engelmann, Peter Keetman, Wulf Mähl, Klaus Oberer, Roland Reimann.

Where not otherwise indicated, all posters and printed matter were printed in Germany.

Format: information follows the sequence height × width, and works in cm.

The history of posters is a new research field – reliable information is rare. Any pointers and additional information are welcome:
plakat.sammlung@museum-gestaltung.ch and
kb@smb.spk-berlin.de

**Advertisements and illustrations by Michael Engelmann appeared in the following magazines, among others:**

Deutsche Medizinische Wochenschrift (1960)
Gebrauchsgraphik (1950, 1957)
Neue Illustrierte (1965)
Quick (1964)
Spiegel (1964)
Stern (1959, 1960, 1964)
Twen (1960 – 1963)

**1** Roth-Händle naturrein
naturally pure
1955
Offset 118,7 × 83,8
B, Z

**2** Roth-Händle naturrein
1963
Offset 118,7 × 82,6
Seriennummer 6357
B, Z

**3** Roth-Händle naturrein
1960
Offset 118,7 × 83,8
und 40,7 × 28,8
Seriennummer 50/60
B, Z

**4** Roth-Händle naturrein
1964
Offset 118,5 × 83,9
und 177,5 × 83,5
Seriennummer 64/2 K
B, Z

**5** Roth-Händle naturrein
1965
Offset 118,8 × 83,9
Seriennummer 11/65
B

**6** Roth-Händle naturrein
1961
Offset 118,7 × 84
Seriennummer 6156
Z

**7** Roth-Händle naturrein
1962
Offset 118,8 × 84 und 177 × 84
Seriennummer 62/34
B, Z

**8** Velocità…sicurezza/pneumatici
Pirelli
Geschwindigkeit… Sicherheit/
Pirelli Reifen
Speed and safety/Pirelli tyres
1952
IT Offset 100 × 69,5
Z

**9** Pirelli/Il pneumatico che
morde la strada
Der Reifen mit Bodenhaftung
The tyre for roadholding
1952
IT Offset 66,6 × 47,8
B, Z

**10** Zuerst T2/dann rasieren/viel
länger glatt – First T2/then
shave/smooth for much longer
1963
Offset 168,2 × 118,8
B, Z

**11** Ausstellung amerikanischer
Architektur im Amerikahaus
1950
Linol- und Buchdruck 86 × 60
Z

**12** Dein Blick in die Welt: Bücher
Your view of the world – books
Foto: Wrubel
1954
Offset 59,2 × 41,8
B

**13** Die Neue Zeitung/
Täglich einmal um die Welt
Once round the world daily
Foto: Amman
1950/51
Offset 83,8 × 58,6
B, Z

**14** Tag des Buches
1959
Offset 59 × 41,8
B, Z

**15** Sicherheit? Ja! – Security?
Yes!/Barmenia Versicherungen
ca. 1960
Offset 119 × 84
B

**16–20** Davosin
Hepaderichol
Benadryl Expectorans
Chlormycetin Succinat
1959/60
Werbedrucksachen für Parke Davis
Offset ca. 33 × 24
B

**21–23** Ambodryl
Ferrostrène
Chloromycetin Ophthalmic
1959/60
Werbekarten für Parke Davis
Offset 21 × 14,7
B

**24** Kieler Woche
[Sailing regatta]
1965
Offset 118,7 × 83,7
und 83,8 × 59,3
B, Z

**25** Fulda Diadem/Wenn's kritisch
wird – When things get critical
1964
Zeitschrifteninserat (Stern 3/1964)
36,4 × 26
B

**26** Chloromycetin Ohrentropfen
1959/60
Werbekarte für Parke Davis
Offset 21 × 14,7
B

**27** Chloromycetin Ophthalmic
Inseratentwurf
1959/60
Zwischenaufnahme, Silbergelatine
30 × 23,8
B

**28** Pirelli/Il pneumatico per tutti
Der Reifen für alle – The tyre for all
1952
IT Offset 100 × 69,5
Z

**29** Potent Optilets
1959
Offset 53,3 × 34,2
B, Z

**30** Sprich Dü-pi-fiss/trink Dupuis
Fils – Say Dü-pi-fiss/drink Dupuis
Fils
ca. 1962
Offset 59,3 × 41,7
B

**31** Schneller mit Brunsviga
Quicker with Brunsviga
1960
Offset 59,4 × 41,9
B

**32–34** Bell Telephone Company
ca. 1958
Serie von 3 Entwürfen. Zwischen-
aufnahmen nach Zeichnungen,
Silbergelatine ca. 41 × 31
B

**35** Hamilton Bond
ca. 1958
Silbergelatine/Collage, schwarze
Tusche 28 × 26,7
B

**36** Auch gebrauchte Volkswagen
mit Garantie – All used
Volkswagens with guarantee
1954/55
Offset 119,7 × 79,6
B, Z

**37** Libella mit Schuss
Libella Top
1959
Offset 118,4 × 83,4
und 83,8 × 59,3
B, Z

**38** Libella/wirklich erfrischend
really refreshing
1959
Offset 118,4 × 83,6 und 83,8 × 59,3
B, Z

**39** Cinzano
1964
Offset 159 × 83,9
B, Z

**40** Grosses Cinzano Preisausschreiben 64/Machen Sie mit!
Competition 64/Just join in!
1964
Offset 168 × 119
B, Z

**41–44** Jacobi schmeckt mit 18 und mit 80/Jacobi 1880
Tastes good at 18 and 80
1963
Serie. Farbfotografie/Collage
ca. 26,7 × 26
B

**45** Danke, o.b./Jetzt fühl' ich mich frei!
Thank you o.b./Now I feel free
[o.b. = tampon]
ca. 1963/64
Farbfotografie (Kodak)/Collage
26,5 × 26
B

**46** Konferenz der Tage-Diebe
The day-thieves' conference/o.b.
ca. 1963/64
Farbfotografie/Collage 26,4 × 26
Privatbesitz

**47–50** Sarotti
ca. 1963/64
Aus einer Serie von 7 Farbfotografien (Kodak)
B

Stempel und Radiergummi
28,2 × 28,6 (40 × 30)
Telefonhörer
30,4 × 30,3 (39,4 × 30,9)
Telefonhörer
27,3 × 26,8 (38,9 × 30,8)
Schraubzwinge
29 × 26,7 (38,7 × 30,2)

**51** Libella
Foto: Peter Keetman
1956
Offset 117,6 × 82,3
B, Z

**52** Good mornings begin with the Inquirer/The Philadelphia Inquirer
Foto: Carl Baker
1958
US Offset 216,1 × 106,7
B, Z

**53** Good mornings begin with the Inquirer/Welcome/
The Philadelphia Inquirer
Foto: Carl Baker
1958
US Offset 215,8 × 106,3
B, Z

**54** Good mornings begin with the Inquirer/daily and Sunday/
The Philadelphia Inquirer
Foto: Carl Baker
1958
US Offset 217 × 106,8
B, Z

**55–58** Im Falle eines Falles klebt Uhu wirklich alles
Broken – never rue it
Uhu's sure to glue it
1957
Anzeigenserie
Offset 14 × 18
Privatbesitz

**59** Das Kinderzimmer
Illustration zu einer Science-Fiction Erzählung von Ray Bradbury
Illustration for a science fiction story by Ray Bradbury
1962
In: Twen 1962, H. 11, Doppelseite 26/27
B

**60** Knud Leif Thomsen:
Die Selbstmörderschule
1965
Filmprogrammheft, Umschlag
Hg. Beta Film GmbH & Co, München
B

**61** Das Testament des Dr. Mabuse
1962
Offset 118,4 × 83,4
und 84 × 59,2
B, Z

**62** Dämmerstunde/Bols Stunde
Twilight hour/Bols hour
1959/1960
Aus einer Anzeigenserie.
Hier aus: Stern 1959, H. 47, S. 71
B

**63** Bols/Gold Top Whisky
ca. 1960
Silbergelatine/Collage
37,6 × 20,7
B

**64** Unverkennbar Bols
Unmistakably Bols
Foto: Hans Engelmann
1959
Offset 171,5 × 118,8
B, Z

**65** Roth-Händle naturrein
1959
Offset 83,5 × 59,5
Seriennummer 29a/59
Z

**66** Roth-Händle naturrein
1958
Offset 118,8 × 83,8
B

**67** Roth-Händle naturrein
1957
Offset 118,9 × 83,8 und 82,6 × 58,7
B

**68** Roth-Händle naturrein
1957
Offset 117,5 × 82,2
B, Z

**69** Roth-Händle naturrein
1959
Offset 118,5 × 83,7
und 83,7 × 58,9
Seriennummer 28/59 und 28a/59
B, Z

**70** Roth-Händle naturrein
1960
Offset 118,5 × 84
Z

**71** Roth-Händle naturrein
1960
Offset 118,4 × 83,8
und 83 × 58,7
Seriennummer 53/60 und 53a/60
B, Z

**72** Roth-Händle naturrein
1960
Offset 119,5 × 83,5
Z

**73** Roth-Händle naturrein
1961
Offset 178 × 84
Seriennummer 6152
B

**74** Roth-Händle naturrein
1961
Offset 176,6 × 84,1
Seriennummer 6151
B, Z

**75** Roth-Händle naturrein
1963
Offset (9x) 84,1 × 118,9 und 119 × 82,5
B, Z

**76** Roth-Händle naturrein
1963
Offset 177,5 × 84
Seriennummer 6354
Z

**77** Roth-Händle naturrein
1963
Offset 177 × 82,3
Seriennummer 6342
B, Z

**78** Roth-Händle naturrein
1963
Offset 121,8 × 83,4
Seriennummer 6351
B, Z

**79** Roth-Händle naturrein
1962
Offset 118,6 × 84
und 178 × 84
Seriennummer 62/23
Z

**80** Roth-Händle naturrein
1962
Offset 118,6 × 84
Seriennummer 62/32
B

**81** Renault R 4L/jetzt DM 4.200
now DM 4,200
1963
Offset 83,6 × 118,6
B, Z

**82** Renault R 8/Hand und
Fuss sind frei
Hand and foot are free
1963
Offset 84,1 × 118,7
B, Z

**83–90** Renault-Serie
1961–63
Offset, Inseratandrucke
ca. 33 × 25, 20 × 40, 30 × 40
B

**91** Roth-Händle naturrein
1964
Offset 118,7 × 83,9
Seriennummer 64/2 I
B, Z

**92** Roth-Händle naturrein
1964
Offset 120,5 × 83,5
Seriennummer 64/2 L
B

**93** Roth-Händle naturrein
1965
Offset 119 × 84
Seriennummer 12/65
B

**94** Roth-Händle naturrein
1965
Offset 118,6 × 84
und 177 × 84
Seriennummer 13/65
B, Z

**95** Roth-Händle naturrein
1965
Offset 118,5 × 84
Seriennummer 14/65
B, Z

**96** Roth-Händle naturrein
1965
Offset 177,2 × 83,4
Seriennummer 4/65
B

**97** Roth-Händle naturrein
1965
Offset 178 × 83,6
Seriennummer 5/65
B, Z

**98** Roth-Händle naturrein
1966
Offset 177,8 × 84
Seriennummer 2/66
B, Z

**99** Roth-Händle naturrein
1966
Offset 177,8 × 83,8 und 118,5 × 84,5
Seriennummer 1/66
B, Z

**100** Roth-Händle naturrein
1966
Offset 177,8 × 83,6 und 118 × 84
Seriennummer 6/66
B, Z

**101** Roth-Händle naturrein
1966
Offset 177,9 × 84
Seriennummer 5/66
B

**102** Roth-Händle naturrein
1966
Offset 118,8 × 83,5
Seriennummer 14/66
B, Z

**103–108** Studien zu Roth-Händle
ca. 1963
Aus einer Serie von 7 Fotografien,
Silbergelatine je ca. 50,5 × 36,5
B

**109** Roth-Händle naturrein
1966
Offset 119,1 × 83,2
Seriennummer 13/66
B, Z

**110** Studie zu Roth-Händle
ca. 1964
Silbergelatine (Kodak) 40 × 30,3
B

**Zusätzliche Bestände in der Kunstbibliothek, Staatliche Museen zu Berlin**

**I. Plakate**

P1 Epoca. 1953
Offset 140,5 × 100,4

P2 Ata Imi Perwoll Persil.
Henkel & Cie. 1953/54
Offset 83,9 × 59,2

P3 Persil, nichts anderes. 1953/54
Offset 83,8 × 58,7

P4 Gebrauchte Volkswagen mit
dem Gütesiegel. 1953
Siebdruck 119,5 × 79,6

P5 Tag des Buches. 1954
Offset 59,3 × 41,9

P6 Roth-Händle naturrein. 1957
Offset 83,7 × 59,2

P7a/7b Roth-Händle naturrein.
1959
Offset 118,7 × 83,6
und 83,2 × 58,6
Seriennummer 27/59 und 27a/59

P8 Roth-Händle naturrein. 1961
Offset 118,9 × 83,7
Seriennummer 6155

P9 Roth-Händle naturrein. 1962
Offset 177,6 × 83,8
Seriennummer 62/24

P10 Sherlock Holmes. 1962
Offset 84,5 × 60.5

P11 Roth-Händle naturrein. 1963
Offset 178,6 × 83,8
Seriennummer 6341

P12 Roth-Händle naturrein. 1964
Offset 119,4 × 84
Seriennummer 64/2 H

P13 Roth-Händle naturrein. 1964
Offset 178,3 × 84
Seriennummer 64/3 A

P14 Roth-Händle naturrein. 1964
Offset 179,3 × 83,7
Foto: Roland Reimann
Seriennummer 64/3 C

P15 Roth-Händle naturrein. 1964
Offset 177,7 × 83,7
Seriennummer 64/3 E

P16 ei ei ei Verpoorten/
meistgekaufter Eierlikör der Welt.
Plakataufsteller
Offset 46 × 33,8

P17 Tapinova. 1965
Offset 117,2 × 83,6

P18 Roth-Händle naturrein. 1964
Offset 178,3 × 84
Seriennummer 1/65

P19 Roth-Händle naturrein. 1965
Offset 177,5 × 83,4
Seriennummer 3/65

P20 Roth-Händle naturrein. 1966
Offset 178 × 83,3
Seriennummer 3/66

P21 Roth-Händle naturrein. 1966
Offset 177,8 × 83,2
Seriennummer 4/66

P22 Roth-Händle naturrein. 1966
Offset 118,7 × 84
Seriennummer 11/66

P23 Roth-Händle naturrein. 1966
Offset 119,1 × 83,2
Seriennummer 12/66

**II. Werbedrucksachen/Inserate**

W1 Lincoln kommt. 1959
Inseratandruck, Offset 32 × 24

W2 Der Mann, der Lincoln raucht. 1959
Inseratdruck, Offset 28,8 × 27,4

W3 Reflex Special. Neuer Name – neues Kleid.
Schreibmaschinenpapier. ca. 1962
Faltbogen 56,9 × 40
(zugeklappt 28,4 × 20 )

W4 T2 vor der Elektrorasur. 1962
Verpackung

W5 T 2. Pré electricshave. 1962
Zündholzbrief

W6 Wilkhan Sitzmöbel. ca. 1963
Prospekt
Foto: Karl Hugo Schmölz

W7 Renault R4 und Fourgonnette. 1963/64, Werbeheft

W8 Diamix
Inserat für Diamalt München. 1963
36,5 × 25,8

W9 Tente-Rollen für alles was rollt!
Faltprospekt
62,4 × 29,8, zugeklappt 29,7 × 20,9

**III. Filmprogramme**

FP1 Susumu Hani: Sie und Er. 1965, Hg. Beta Film GmbH & Co, München

FP2 Nico Papatakis: Les Abysses. 1964, Hg. Beta Film GmbH & Co, München

**IV. Entwürfe**
**Fotos und Fotocollagen**

F1 Volkswagen. ca. 1954
Silbergelatine 42 × 58,2

*F2–F24 Roth-Händle naturrein. 1956–1964*

F2 Roth-Händle naturrein
Silbergelatine getönt/Collage
29,9 × 23,9

F3 Roth-Händle naturrein
Silbergelatine getönt/Collage
29,8 × 23,8

F4 Roth-Händle naturrein
Rundbild, Farbfotografie (Kodak)
26 cm Durchmesser

F5 Hand mit Zigarette
Silbergelatine 39,1 × 29,8

F6 Roth-Händle naturrein
Silbergelatine/Collage 26,9 × 12

F7 Kopf, Hand und Zigarette
Silbergelatine getönt/Collage
30 × 23,8

F8 Roth-Händle naturrein
(Packung und Zitrone)
Farbfotografie 39,5 × 29,9

F9–F11 Roth-Händle naturrein
(Serie für Inserat) Jeweils Silbergelatine, teilweise getönt
F9: 37,5 × 26,7/F10: 38,8 × 27,2/
F11: 33,8 × 24,2

F12 Roth-Händle naturrein
Silbergelatine/Collage getönt
59,5 × 28,3

F13 Männerkopf, Hand und Zigarette
Silbergelatine, getönt 59 × 49,7

F14 Männerkopf, Hand und Zigarette
Silbergelatine 56,9 × 37,4

F15 Roth-Händle naturrein
Silbergelatine und Farbfotografie/
Collage 39,5 × 18,5

F16 Hand mit Zigarette
Folge. Kontaktbogen,
Silbergelatine 24 × 29,7

F17 Hand mit Zigarette
Folge. Kontaktbogen,
Silbergelatine 24 × 29,7

F18 Hand mit Zigaretten
Folge von vier Aufnahmen.
Kontaktbogen, Silbergelatine
17,9 × 12,1

F19 Hand mit Männerbildnis, rauchend
Silbergelatine (Kodak) 40 × 30,2

F20 Hand und Männerporträt mit Bart, rauchend
Silbergelatine (Kodak) 33 × 22

F21 Bildnis Bob Hyde, rauchend
Silbergelatine (Kodak) 39,8 × 30,3

F22 Hand und Männerbildnis, rauchend
Silbergelatine (Kodak) 41,1 × 21,7

F23 Hand und Porträt eines jungen Mannes, rauchend
Silbergelatine (Kodak) 40 × 19,5

F24 Hand und Frauenbildnis
Silbergelatine (Kodak) 40,4 × 20,6

F25 Benadryl Expectorans. 1960
Sein Auftritt ist gerettet
Silbergelatine/Collage 38,1 × 38

F26 Hepaderichol schützt die kranke Leber. 1960
Silbergelatine/Collage 48,5 × 35,3

F27 Bols. Alter Weinbrand mit Soda. ca. 1960
Silbergelatine/Collage 16,3 × 39,4

F28 Glas mit perlender Flüssigkeit
Silbergelatine 23,1 × 17,1 (24 × 18)

F29 Omega. 1960
Für eine Anzeigenserie
Silbergelatine 28,7 × 26,7

F30 Hand mit Uhr
Silbergelatine 20,7 × 13,6

F31–34 Omega
Serie von 4 Fotografien
Silbergelatine ca. 35,5 × 29,5

F35 Ferrari
Farbfotografie 36,4 × 26,2

F36–F40 Jopa. Serie. 1961
Jeweils Farbfotografie (Kodak)/
Collage ca. 36,5 × 19,5

F41 Jopa (ohne Text)
Farbfotografie (Kodak) 40,3 × 30,3

F42 Burger 10
Endlich ein naturfarbenes Zigarillo zum Zigarettenpreis
Silbergelatine/Collage
58,7 × 39,5

F43 Frau mit Kognakschwenker. 1962
(Inseratentwurf, wahrscheinlich für Jacobi)
Silbergelatine/Collage 23,8 × 25,3

F44 Hand mit Kognakschwenker
Farbfotografie (Kodak) 23,9 × 23,3

F45 Renault/Encore une idée ingénieuse de Renault. 1963
Farbfotografie/Collage 36 × 26,5

F46 Renault Dauphine. 1963
Silbergelatine/Collage 33,8 × 25,2

F47 Encore une idée ingénieuse de Renault. 1963
Farbfotografie/Collage 36 × 26,5

F48 Aral Super. 1963/64
Farbfotografie/Collage 32,4 × 29,3

F49 Picon/Paris, wie es wirklich ist, ist in ihrem Glas!
Farbfotografie/Collage 36,5 × 26,4

F50 Cinzano/Weil Sie Stiefmütterchen nicht trinken können. 1964
Farbfotografie und Textcollage
36,5 × 26,5

F51 Cinzano. 1964
Farbfotografie (Kodak)
35,6 × 26,7 (39,2 × 30)
Entwurf für Inseratserie

F52 Sunkist/California Lemon juice
Farbfotografie/Collage 36,5 × 26,5

F53–55 Jägermeister (Serie)
Jeweils Farbfotomontage (Kodak)
40,5 × 30,5

F56 Ballantines
Silbergelatine/Collage 37 × 24,6

F57 Apfel
Farbfotografie (Kodak) 39,7 × 30

F58 Ravensburger Spiele.
2 Varianten (grün und blau)
Farbfotografie (Kodak)
und Textcollage je 38,7 × 27

F59 Eduscho Gala (Kaffeetasse)
Mit Milch oder ohne
Farbfotografie (Kodak)/Collage
36,3 × 26,6

F60 Kaffeetasse (Eduscho)
Farbfotografie
24 × 18,9 (28,5 × 19,7)

F61 Eduscho Gala. Sind Sie schon dabei?
Farbfotografie/Collage 36,5 × 27

F62 Gasolin Super. ca. 1964/65
Ring frei für die nächste Runde...
Farbfotografie/Collage 36,5 × 26,3

F63 Gasolin Record
Farfotografie (Kodak) 39,1 × 20,4
(39,5 × 20,5)

F64–F67 Tobler. Serie. ca. 1965
Farbfotografien (Kodak)
F64: 40,8 × 30,8/F65: 36,3 × 27/
F66: Tobler-o-rum, 36,4 × 26,1/
F67: Tobler (Nuss), 36,2 × 26

F68 Tobler/Wann haben Sie zum letzten Mal Schokolade gegessen?
Silbergelatine/Collage 29,7 × 21

F69 Evidur. Wäsche-Steife
Farbfotografie(Collage) 27,3 × 27
Inseratentwurf, Verwendet wurde ein beliebiger Text. Hier: zu Renault

F70 Balatred. Fussbodenbelag
«Sie» und «Er» sind sich einig
Farbfotografie und Textcollage
36,4 × 26,3

F71 Balatred. Fussbodenbelag.
Ob in Schweden – ob in der Schweiz. Farbfotografie und Textcollage, 36,3 × 26,4

F72 Balatred extra
Farbfotografie, 40,2 × 30,3
(40,6 × 31)

F73 Odina. Quellfrisch
Farbfotografie/Collage 35,7 × 25,2

F74 Gläser vor Kühlschrank (Bosch) Silbergelatine 30 × 23,8

F75 Milchflaschen (Bosch)
Farbfotografie (Kodak) 39 × 30,2

F76 Tapinova. 1965
Farbfotografie (Kodak) 37 × 26,8

F77 Tura Canday wissen Sie einen guten Namen? (Henkel)
Farbfotografie/Collage 36,2 × 26,2

F78 Hier macht Henkel Freizeit flüssig
Farbfotomontage 36,5 × 26,4

F79–F81 Rawe.
Serie von drei Modellen
Silbergelatine je ca. 39,7 × 30

F82 Coca Cola
Farbfotografie (Kodak) 36,5 × 26

F83 Galama/Weil Sie Stiefmütterchen nicht trinken können
Farbfotografie (Kodak)/Collage
27,8 × 26,5

F84 o.b.
Farbfotografie (Kodak) 36 × 30,1
(40,6 × 30,8)

F85 Tage-Dieb/Nehmen Sie o.b., dann sind die kritischen Tage wie weggestohlen
Silbergelatine/Collage 26,4 × 26

F86 Verpoorten. Um 1964
Farbfotografie (Kodak) 36,3 × 26,8
(40,2 × 31)

F87–F88 Paar (Phillips Rasierapparat) Silbergelatine je ca. 40 × 30

F89–F104 Paris-Serie (Paare).
Fotostudien. Kontaktbögen,
Silbergelatine je ca. 27,8 × 22,2

F105 Männerkopf mit Hut (für T2)
Silbergelatine 30,4 × 23,8

**V. Zeichnungen**

Z1 Total/Erst total tanken, dann gemsenflink bergauf. Bleistift auf Transparentpapier 19 × 34,8

Z2 Total lässt Ihren Pferden freien Lauf. Bleistift auf Transparentpapier 19 × 35,4

Z3–11 Greer Williams: Männer gegen Krebs und Polio
Serie von 9 Buchumschlagentwürfen, 1959/60:
Tempera und Lackfarbe jeweils ca. 22 × 16 (nicht realisiert)

*Z12–Z18 Lincoln. 1959/60*

Z12 Bleistift 27,2 × 18,5 (43,6 × 31,4)

Z13 Mann mit Pfeife
Bleistift, Tusche, Folie 25,5 × 18,2

Z14 Schlagzeuger
Bleistift 27,3 × 19 (44 × 31,2)

Z15 Beleuchter
Bleistift 25,5 × 24,5 (44 × 31,3)

Z 16 Beleuchter, Variante
Bleistift 25,8 × 24,8 (44 × 31,3)

Z17–Z18 Studienblätter Lincoln
je Bleistift 29,5 × 21

Z19–Z22 Studienblätter King
Bleistift
Z19: 26,2 × 34,8/Z20: 33,8 × 24,3/
Z21: 25,9 × 36,3/Z22: 33,5 × 23,8

**Literatur**

Allgemeines Künstlerlexikon, München, Leipzig 2002, Bd. 34.

Allgemeines Lexikon der Bildenden Künstler des 20. Jahrhunderts, Hans Vollmer, Hg., Leipzig, Bd. 5.

Art Directors Club für Deutschland, Hg., 1. Art Directors Annual für Werbung und Zeitschriften, Düsseldorf 1965, Nr. 74.

Art Directors Club New York, Hg., 38th Annual of Advertising and Editorial Art, New York 1959.

Amstutz, Walter, Hg., Who's Who in Graphic Art, Zürich 1962.

Barthel, Tobias M., Photo Graphik International, München 1965.

«Beste deutsche Plakate», in: Gebrauchsgraphik 1954, H. 8, S. 4; 1956, H. 8, S. 18; 1957, H. 8, S. 3; 1958, H. 8, S. 43; 1959, H. 8, S. 6; 1960, H. 8, S. 15; 1961, H. 9, S. 5; 1963, H. 8, S. 8; 1964, H. 8; S. 5, 11; 1965, H. 8, S. 3; 1966, H. 8, S. 2, 6; Graphik 1953, H. 6, S. 327; 1954; H. 7, S. 387; 1956, H. 8, S. 429; Format 1965, H. 3, S. 39; 1966, H. 7, S. 44, 45.

Ernst, Jupp und Karl Oskar Blase, documenta III, 1964, Industrial Design Graphic, Kassel 1964.

Dorén, Gustav Nils, Das Cigarettenplakat im Laufe der Reemtsma-Firmengeschichte. Sonderdruck aus dem Geschäftsbericht 1974 der Reemtsma Cigarettenfabriken GmbH Hamburg, Hamburg 1974.

Duvigneau, Volker, Zwischen Kaltem Krieg und Wirtschaftswunder. Deutsche und europäische Plakate 1945–1959, München 1982.

Friedl, Friedrich, Nicolaus Ott und Bernard Stein, Typographie: wann, wer, wie, Köln 1998.

Gerstner, Karl und Markus Kutter, Die neue Graphik, Teufen 1959.

Graphis Annual, International Yearbook of Advertising Art, Zürich 1959/60, S. 32; 1966, S. 145.

Hollis, Richard, Graphic Design, A Concise History, London 1994.

International Poster Annual 1956/57, S. 70; 1958/59, S. 61, 63, 115; 1965/66, S. 63; 1967/68, S. 63.

Johnson, J. Stewart, The Modern American Poster, Kyoto, New York 1983.

Koetzle, Michael, Hg., Twen. Revision einer Legende, München 1995.

Koetzle, Michael und Carsten M. Wolff, Fleckhaus. Deutschlands erster Art Director, München, Berlin 1997.

Krause, Jürgen, Hg., Die nützliche Moderne, Münster 2000.

Kühnel, Anita, Die Poesie des Konkreten, Graphik und Plakate der Kasseler Schule, Berlin 2000.

Kunstgewerbemuseum der Stadt Zürich, Meister der Plakatkunst, Zürich 1959.

Kutter, Markus, Werbung in der Schweiz. Geschichte einer unbekannten Branche, Zürich 1983.

Le Coultre, Martijn F. und Alston W. Purvis, A Century of Posters, Blaricum 2002.

Le Coultre, Martijn F. und Alston W. Purvis, Graphic Design 20th Century, Amsterdam 2003.

Müller-Brockmann, Josef und Karl Wobmann, Fotoplakate. Von den Anfängen bis zur Gegenwart, Aarau, Stuttgart 1989.

Photographis, International Annual of Advertising Photography, 1966, S. 41, 83, 134; 1967, S. 149, 185, 187.

Popitz, Klaus, 25 Jahre Filmplakate in Deutschland, Berlin 1975.

Rademacher, Hellmut, Das deutsche Plakat von den Anfängen bis zur Gegenwart, Dresden 1965.

Sailer, Anton, Das Plakat. Geschichte, Stil und gezielter Einsatz eines unentbehrlichen Werbemittels, München 1965.

Schmalriede, Manfred, Deutsche, Werbefotografie 1925–1988, Stuttgart 1989.

Schmalriede, Manfred und Ute Eskildsen, Fotografie und Werbung. Werbefotografie in Deutschland seit den zwanziger Jahren, Essen 1989.

Schmidt-Rhen, Helmut und Helfried Hagenberg, Hg., Michael Engelmann. Plakate von 1951 bis 1966. Eine Retrospektive, Düsseldorf 1983.

Spielmann, Heinz, Internationale Plakate 1871–1971, München 1971.

Thompson, Philip und Peter Davenport, The Dictionary of Visual Language, Harmondsworth 1980.

Werbung in Deutschland. Jahrbuch der deutschen Werbung, Düsseldorf 1964, S. 138, 177–180, 258/59; 1965, S. 146–147.

Westag Werbeagentur, Hg., Renault-Werbung. Ein Querschnitt durch die Anzeigenwerbung für die Deutsche Renault 1962/63, Köln 1963.

Wichmann, Hans, Warenplakate. Meisterplakate von der Jahrhundertwende bis heute, München 1981.

Villani, Dino, Storia del manifesto pubblicitario, Mailand 1964.

Weill, Alain, Le design graphique, Paris 2003.

**Zeitschriftenaufsätze / Rezensionen:**

Domus, H. 437, April 1966.

Form 102, 1983, H. 2, S. 35–37.

Format 1967, H. 11, S. 87.

Gebrauchsgraphik 1950, H. 10, S. 11–14; 1954, H. 3, S. 134–146; H. 6, S. 10; 1955, H. 7, S. 4–11; 1957, H. 6, S. 16–19; 1957, H. 9, S. 10–13; 1960, H. 1, S. 10–17; 1961, H. 9, S. 34 –41; 1962, H. 5, S. 16–25; 1964, H. 1, S. 2–9; 1965, H. 1, S. 10; H. 5, S. 2–11; 1989, H. 10, S. 20–37.

Graphik 1954, H. 2, S. 72; H. 3, S. 136; 1961, H. 7, S. 26–30; H. 10, S. 6–8; 1965, H. 1, S. 12–17.

W&V, Werben und Verkaufen, H. 14, 1972.

**Pavel Michael Engelmann**

Geboren am 26. Februar 1928 in Prag als Sohn des Chemikers und Kunstseidefabrikanten Walter Engelmann und der Schauspielerin Sonik Rainer, die im Berlin der 1930er Jahre Karriere macht. Entwurzelte Kindheit durch die Scheidung der Eltern und ihren Streit um das Sorgerecht. Schule in Hohenelbe bei Prag unter der Obhut des Vaters. Enteignung des Vaters aufgrund seiner jüdischen Herkunft. 1940 Flucht aus dem Sudetenland und 1941 Emigration in die USA mit dem Vater. Hier lebt Engelmann bis 1949 in New York. Mit verschiedenen Jobs verdient er sich seinen Lebensunterhalt, bevor er 1946/47 in die US-Army eintritt und in Linz/Österreich stationiert wird. Im April 1947 Rückkehr nach New York. Abbruch einer Schauspielausbildung, um in einem Grafikstudio zu arbeiten. November 1949 Erlangung der amerikanischen Staatsbürgerschaft.

Von Dezember 1949 bis Juni 1950 arbeitet er in Amsterdam für die Zeitschrift international textiles, danach bis August 1952 als Art Director der US-amerikanischen Tageszeitung Die Neue Zeitung in München. Hier beginnt die Zusammenarbeit mit dem Fotografen Peter Keetman. August 1952 bis Oktober 1953 Aufenthalt in Mailand. Arbeiten für das Studio «sigla», die Zeitschrift Epoca und das Industrieunternehmen Pirelli.

Oktober 1953 bis November 1954 Atelier in Düsseldorf. Werbearbeiten für Henkel und Volkswagen. Ab 1954 Atelier in München. 1955 Beginn der Zusammenarbeit mit Roth-Händle. Aufenthalt in New York von August 1957 bis Dezember 1958. Aufträge für CBS und The Philadelphia Inquirer. Das American Institute of Graphic Arts (AIGA) ernennt Engelmanns Inserate zu den «besten des Jahres 1957». Ab Ende 1958 wieder mehrheitlich in München. Mitinitiator der Gruppe novum, deren Mitglied er aber nicht wird. 1959 Certificate of Merit vom ADC New York. Spätestens seit 1955 enge Verbindungen zu Basel, wo er für den Pharmakonzern J. R. Geigy AG arbeitet. Freundschaftliche Kontakte zu Armin Hofmann, der an der Allgemeinen Gewerbeschule Basel unterrichtet, sowie zu dessen ehemaligem Schüler Karl Gerstner. Das neu gegründete Atelier Gerstner+Kutter (später GGK) publiziert 1959 Werke von Engelmann in seinem Manifest «die neue Graphik», 1959. In München Aufträge für Bols, teilweise mit Assistenz der Absolventen der Baseler Grafikklasse Pierre Mendell und Klaus Oberer, bevor diese 1961 das Studio Mendell & Oberer gründen. Im Auftrag der Werbeagentur Westag, Köln, seit 1961 Renault-Werbung und Zusammenarbeit mit dem Texter Helmuth Hartmann. In den frühen 1960er Jahren zahlreiche Auszeichnungen für Anzeigen und Plakate. 14. Juli 1964 Gründung der Werbeagentur Engelmann, Hartmann, Dr. Wanner in Düsseldorf, die bereits am 1. Juni 1965 wieder aufgelöst wird. Am 24. Januar 1966 Freitod in Düsseldorf.

**Pavel Michael Engelmann**

Born on 26 February 1928 in Prague as the son of the chemist Walter Engelmann and Sonik Rainer, an actress who made a career in 1930s Berlin. Uprooted as a child by his parents' divorce and their dispute about custody. School in Hohenelbe near Prague while in his father's care. Father dispossessed because of his Jewish origins. Fled from the Sudetenland in 1940 and emigrated to the USA in 1941 with his father. Engelmann lived in New York until 1949. He earned his living by doing various jobs before starting military service with the US Army in 1946/47, being stationed in Linz, Austria. Returned to New York in April 1947. Broke off training as an actor to work in a graphic arts studio. Granted American citizenship in November 1949. From December 1949 to June 1950 he worked in Amsterdam for the international textiles magazine. After that he came to Munich, where he was Art Director of the US-American daily paper Die Neue Zeitung until August 1952. Here he started working with the photographer Peter Keetman. In Milan from August 1952 to October 1953. Created work for the "sigla" studio, the magazine Epoca and the Pirelli industries.

Studio in Düsseldorf from October 1953 to November 1954. Advertising work for firms including Henkel and Volkswagen. Studio in Munich from 1954. Here work with Roth-Händle started in 1955. In New York from August 1957 to December 1958. Commissions for CBS and The Philadelphia Inquirer. The American Institute of Graphic Arts (AIGA) names Engelmann's advertisements as the "best of 1967". From late 1958 mostly in Munich again. Co-initiator of the group novum, but does not become a member. Certificate of Merit from the ADC New York in 1959. Close contacts with Basel from 1955 at the latest, where he works for the pharmaceutical firm J.R. Geigy AG. Friendly contact with Armin Hofmann, who teaches at the Allgemeine Gewerbeschule Basel, and with Hofmann's former student Karl Gerstner. The newly founded Gerstner + Kutter studio (later GGK) published works by Engelmann in its 1959 "the new graphic art" manifesto. In Munich work for Bols, partially with the assistance of Pierre Mendell and Klaus Oberer, graduates of the Basel graphic arts class, before the last two found the Mendell + Oberer studio in 1961. Work for the Westag, Cologne advertising agency, Renault advertising from 1961 and start of co-operation with the advertisement copywriter Helmuth Hartmann. Numerous awards for advertisements and posters in the early sixties. Engelmann, Hartmann, Dr. Wanner advertising agency founded in Düsseldorf on 14 July 1964; it is dissolved on 1 June 1965, however. Committed suicide in Düsseldorf on 24 January 1966.

110
**Studie zu Roth-Händle**
ca. 1964

**Anita Kühnel**
Geboren 1951, Studium der Kunstgeschichte an der Humboldt-Universität Berlin. Seit 1978 tätig bei den Staatlichen Museen zu Berlin, zunächst im Kupferstichkabinett als wissenschaftliche Mitarbeiterin. Seit 1992 Kuratorin der Sammlung Plakat- und Reklamekunst der Kunstbibliothek. Promotion 1994.

**Anita Kühnel**
Born 1951, studied art history at the Humboldt-Universität Berlin. Worked for the Staatliche Museen zu Berlin from 1978, first as an academic assistant in the Kupferstichkabinett. Curator of the Kunstbibliothek's Sammlung Plakat- und Reklamekunst since 1992. Doctorate in 1994.

**Felix Studinka**
Geboren 1965 in Zürich. Studium der Kunstwissenschaft, Filmwissenschaft und Ostasiatischen Kunstgeschichte in Zürich. Seit 1997 Kurator der Plakatsammlung des Museums für Gestaltung Zürich.

**Felix Studinka**
Born 1965 in Zurich. Studied art history, cinema studies and Chinese and Japanese art history in Zurich. Curator of the Museum für Gestaltung Zürich's Poster Collection since 1997.

**Stefan Zweifel**
Geboren 1967 in Zürich. Studium der Philosophie, Komparatistik und Ägyptologie in Zürich. Dissertation mit der Studie Pornosophie & Imachination: Sade – La Mettrie – Hegel (Ko-Autor Michael Pfister). Lebt als Sade-Übersetzer und Publizist in Zürich.

**Stefan Zweifel**
Born 1967 in Zurich. Studied philosophy, comparistics and Egyptology in Zurich. Dissertation in the form of the the study Pornosophie & Imachination: Sade – La Mettrie – Hegel (co-author Michael Pfister). Lives as Sade translator and journalist in Zurich.

**Dank**
Viele Personen haben zur Publikation beigetragen.
Wir bedanken uns ganz besonders bei:

**Thanks**
Many people have contributed to this publication.
We would particularly like to thank:

Echo Engelmann
Natascha Engelmann
Hans Ulrich Engelmann
Karl Gerstner
Hans Hillmann
Armin Hofmann
Peter Keetman
Markus Kutter
Pierre Mendell
Klaus Oberer

**«Poster Collection»**
Herausgegeben von / Published by
Felix Studinka
Kurator der Plakatsammlung
Curator of the Poster Collection
Museum für Gestaltung Zürich
In Zusammenarbeit mit / in cooperation with
Bettina Richter, Wissenschaftliche Mitarbeiterin / Scientific collaborator
Christina Reble, Publikationen / Publications
Museum für Gestaltung Zürich

**Michael Engelmann**
Konzept, Redaktion / Concept, Editing:
Anita Kühnel, Felix Studinka, Christina Reble
Gestaltung / Design:
Integral Lars Müller / Hendrik Schwantes
Fotografie/Photography: Jens Ziehe,
Dietmar Katz (Berlin); Franz Xaver Jaggy (Zürich)
Lektorat / Sub-editing: Mark Welzel
Übersetzung / Translation: Michael Robinson
Lithografie / Repro: Ast & Jakob AG, Köniz
Druck / Printing: Vetsch + Co AG, Köniz
Einband / Binding: Buchbinderei Burkhardt AG, Mönchaltorf



Museum für Gestaltung Zürich
Plakatsammlung / Poster Collection
Limmatstrasse 57
CH-8005 Zürich / Switzerland
e-mail: plakat.sammlung@museum-gestaltung.ch
http://www.museum-gestaltung.ch

Staatliche Museen zu Berlin
Kunstbibliothek
Matthäikirchplatz 6
D-10785 Berlin
e-mail: kb@smb.spk-berlin.de
http://www.smpk.de/kb

Lars Müller Publishers
CH–5401 Baden / Switzerland
e-mail: books@lars-muller.ch
http://www.lars-muller-publishers.com

ISBN 3-03778-039-8
Erste Auflage / First Edition 2004

Printed in Switzerland